Communicate

DAVID PAUL

book 2

Language Syllabus

1 Meeting a friend

- describing personal situations
- passing on news about acquaintances
- discussing work and school

2 Plans and dreams

- future (*will*)
- *probably, may, might*
- *wish, hope*

3 Too • Enough

- *too* + adjective, adjective + *enough*
- verb + *too much*, verb + *enough*
- making suggestions

4 Verb + ing • Verb + to

- verbs followed by *-ing*: *miss, hate*, etc.
- verbs followed by *to*: *want, need*, etc.

5 Opinions and beliefs

- *What's ... like? What do you think of ...?*
- giving balanced opinions
- discussing beliefs

6 Describing places

- describing neighborhoods, cities, countries
- *too many, too much*
- *aren't enough, isn't enough*

7 Past continuous

- describing what people were doing
- expressing purpose using *to*
- making accusations

8 Comparatives

- *(not) as ... as ...*
- *not as much, more than*

9 Describing trends

- describing personal changes
- describing economic and social changes
- explaining graphs

10 Superlatives

- adjective + *-est, most* + adjective
- *Which ... do you like best?*
- *Who do you think's the most ..., -est ...?*

11 Present perfect (1)

- recounting experiences
- *Have you ever ...?*
- making invitations

12 Present perfect (2)

- recently completed actions
- recent actions which are still continuing
- *for, since*

13 Present perfect (3)

- application and extension
- contrasting with the past simple
- describing changes

14 Reported speech (1)

- arguing and correcting
- how to switch tenses
- reporting without switching tenses

15 Interested • Interesting

- *-ed* to describe feelings
- *-ing* to describe how things make us feel
- describing appearances

16 Used to

- regular activities in the past
- contrasting the past and present
- using *before* with *used to*

Language Syllabus

17 Tag questions

- questions which assume positive answers
- checking information
- expressing anger

18 Time clauses (1)

- using *when* to link two simultaneous events
- using *when* to link two consecutive events
- describing a sickness or injury

19 Time clauses (2)

- combining *when* with *used to* and *could*
- *until, as soon as*
- talking about ability

20 Noun clauses

- clauses as objects of know, wonder ...
- indirect questions
- reporting that something is lost

21 Conditionals (1)

- *If* sentences (probable conditions)
  If + present ... *will* ...

22 Conditionals (2)

- answering questions with *If* ...
- using *It depends on*
- using two present tenses

23 Giving reasons

- using *because, if* ...
- explaining using *helps, stops, gives,* etc.
- answering a succession of *why* questions

24 Reported speech (2)

- *tell, report, ask,* etc.
- indirect questions
- commands and requests

25 Conditionals (3)

- *If* sentences (improbable conditions)
  If + past ... *would* ...

26 Passives

- the passive form of simple tenses
- prepositions with passive verbs
- *should* + passive infinitives

27 Relative clauses

- relative clauses which define a noun
- relative pronouns: *which, who, where, that*
- giving definitions

28 Should have • Would have

- *should (n't) have, would (n't) have* ...
- *If* sentences referring to the past
- speculation, using *could, might, can't*

29 Impressions

- making deductions using *must, must have*
- *seems, looks like,* etc.
- making sentences with similes

30 Discussions

- comparing cultures
- explaining customs
- discussing the state of the world

One way of teaching a unit

There is no "right" way to use *Communicate*. Every teacher has a different style and every learning situation has its own unique requirements. The following way of teaching each section of a unit provides suggestions for teachers using the course for the first time. The aim is not to be prescriptive, but to suggest methods which can be successfully adapted to individual teaching styles and students' needs.

Note: The language and structures in *Communicate 2* build on the basics learned in *Communicate 1*. When teaching a unit it may be necessary to spend some time reviewing targets taught in the previous level. Guidance on specific review activities is provided in *Communicate 2 Teacher's Book*.

Lead-in

Aims: the introduction of new words and structures; the presentation of these new words and structures in short dialogues where they are linked with language the students already know.

Go through the following sequence with each dialogue/paragraph:

1. Warm-up activity

Use one or more of the warm-up activities from the Teacher's Book. Warm-ups help "create a need" for the target words and structures, and enable the students to feel they are discovering this new language for themselves. Put the students in situations where they either need the target words and structures to express themselves, or where they need to guess the meaning of these structures. The students can then continue this activity among themselves (either as a group or in pairs).

2. Listening (option)

Before playing the cassette or reading to the students, ask them one or two questions to focus on while listening. After finishing the dialogue/paragraph, ask the students for the answers to your questions. Either play the cassette or read again and follow up with comprehension/personalization questions, or go straight to the reading stage. If there is a comprehension stage, either you can ask questions or the students can ask each other the questions in the workbook.

3. Reading

The students take roles or read in turn. Follow this up with comprehension/personalization questions. Either you can ask questions or the students can ask each other the questions in the workbook. These questions sometimes lead into a pairwork activity (see the Teacher's Book for ideas).

Language Builder

Aim: to focus on key grammar and usage targets of the unit.

Personalization

The students make individual sentences which include the words or structures highlighted in blue text. These sentences should be about themselves, their family, their city, their country, or something else they can genuinely relate to.

Controlled practice

Aim: the consolidation of one of the new structures through the controlled use of picture prompts.

Making sentences

The students look at the first picture and read what is written below it. Then, either individually or as a class, they try to make similar sentences, or questions and answers, about the other pictures.

Follow-up practice

Aim: to use a humorous dialogue as a model for either a role-play or self expression. This section provides the link between the previous three sections where the teacher is more in evidence, and the *Communication Activities* where the teacher takes a back seat.

1. Warm-up activity

Use one or more of the warm-up activities from the Teacher's Book. The students can then continue this activity among themselves.

2. Listening (option)

Before playing the cassette or reading to the students, ask them one or two questions to focus on while listening. After finishing the dialogue/paragraph, ask the students for the answers to your questions.

One way of teaching a unit

3. Reading

The students take roles or read in turn.

4. Pair practice

The students do the pairwork activity which is explained (for the teacher) at the bottom of the page. If necessary, help one pair demonstrate what to do in front of the class. Ideally, the students should do an imaginative role-play, but with some classes it may be best not to try this too soon. The extent to which you should be involved will also vary from class to class, but the more you can step back the better, so that the students are better prepared for the *Communication Activities*.

Communication Activities

Aim: to encourage the students to use the new words and structures in activities where they are completely relaxed and having a lot of fun. The first two activities in this section can be done without special equipment; the third activity requires photocopiable material from the Teacher's Book.

The globe symbol indicates an activity with a geographical or cultural focus.

1. Setting up the activity

The students look at the picture of one of the activities and try to guess what to do. Help when necessary. If you are unsure how to do the activity, refer to the Teacher's Book. If the students come up with different ways of doing the activity, don't change what they are doing unless the language targets are not being practiced enough.

2. Total involvement

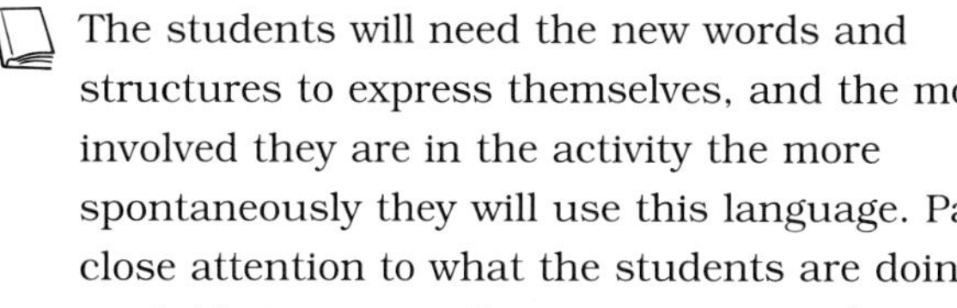

The students will need the new words and structures to express themselves, and the more involved they are in the activity the more spontaneously they will use this language. Pay close attention to what the students are doing, be available to answer their questions, and gently correct when necessary. Try not to interrupt the flow of the activity or reduce their involvement.

Consolidation Exercises

Aim: the consolidation of the new words and structures through personalized sentences. These exercises can either be done orally or in writing.

1. Oral practice

The students can either do all the exercises orally, or just some, in preparation for writing.

2. Writing (option)

If the students are going to write their answers, have them practice orally first, so that all of them clearly understand what to do. They can then write their answers either at home or in class.

The Workbook

The first part of each unit in the workbook has comprehension/ personalization questions which can be used for checking reading or listening comprehension. These questions can be used by the students in class (by themselves or in pairs) or at home. The second part of each unit contains puzzles. The aim of these puzzles is to increase the students' motivation and involvement, and to deepen their understanding of the usage of the new words and structures.

The Cassette/CD

A cassette or audio CD contains all the dialogues/paragraphs in the *Lead-in* and *Follow-up* sections. These can either be used by the teacher in class, or by the student at home in combination with the Workbook.

The Teacher's Book

Contains a step-by-step guide on how to teach each unit and provides the photocopiable material necessary for the third activity in each *Communication Activities* section.

Nationality: Mexican
Occupation: Civil servant

Nationality: Mexican
Occupation: Lawyer

Nationality: Japanese
Occupation: Stewardess

Nationality: Korean
Occupation: Businessman

Nationality: Chinese
Occupation: Doctor

Nationality: Brazilian
Occupation: Artist

Nationality: French
Occupation: Rock singer

Nationality: American
Occupation: English teacher

Nationality: Swiss
Occupation: Student

Nationality: Thai
Occupation: Businesswoman

Nationality: Turkish
Occupation: Student

Meeting a friend 1

Lead-in What are you doing these days?

Michelle: Hello, Sachiko. It's good to see you again. What are you doing these days?

Sachiko: I'm still working as a stewardess. How about you?

Michelle: I'm still an exchange student.

Sachiko: Are you enjoying it?

Michelle: Not very much. I'm thinking of going back to Switzerland.

Sachiko: I'm looking forward to seeing everybody again.

Michelle: Yes, me too.

Sachiko: I heard that Paula and Lee got married.

Michelle: That's great news!

Sachiko: But Manuel and Carmen aren't speaking to each other.

Michelle: That's not surprising!

Language Builder

Kim's still working hard every day.

Carmen's looking forward to playing tennis with Emel.

David and Sachiko are thinking of getting engaged.

Controlled practice These days

1 Michelle's studying for an exam.

2 Kim's ________________ every night.

3 Carmen's ________________ a lot of tennis.

4 Lee and Paula are ________________ a house.

5 Marc's ________________ a new album.

6 Sachiko's ________________ the gym a lot.

Follow-up practice The pay's good

Policeman: What are you doing these days?

Robber: I'm still doing the same job.

Policeman: Are you enjoying it?

Robber: Yes, very much. The pay's good. And I do a lot of running, so it's very healthy. How's your work going?

Policeman: It's not bad. The pay's not very good. But I get a nice car.

Robber: Well, I have to be going now. Give me a call sometime.

Policeman: When's a good time to call you?

Robber: I'm usually home after the banks close.

Pair practice

The students use the ideas in the dialogue as a basis for asking about each others' work or school. They either give true answers or play the roles of famous people.

A. Telling lies
I'm a professional soccer player.
No, you aren't.
You're a civil servant.
B. Interviewing a superstar
What are you doing at the moment?
I'm making a new movie.
C. Who am I?
Photocopiable
Did I get married last year?
No, you didn't.
Bill Clinton
Napoleon Bonaparte
Julius Caesar

1 Consolidation Exercises

1. Reacting

Your best friend got engaged last week.

That's great news!

One of your friends is in the hospital.

Your English teacher is moving to another school.

There's an alien in your living room.

2. News

I heard that

I heard that

3. What are they thinking of doing?

a. She's thinking of getting a motorcycle.

b.

c.

d.

e.

f.

Questionnaire

What are you doing these days?

What are you thinking of doing tomorrow?

How's your work/school going?

When's a good time to call you?

Plans and dreams 2

Lead-in Do you think you'll win?

Kim: What are you going to do this summer?

Emel: I'm going to study hard! And I'm going to play a lot of tennis. Carmen and I are going to play in a doubles tournament.

Kim: Do you think you'll win?

Emel: I don't know, but I think we'll do OK. Carmen's a pretty good player.

Emel: How about you? What are you going to do?

Kim: Well, I'm not going to study very hard! I won't have time!

Emel: Are you going to go on any business trips?

Kim: Yes, I'll probably go back to Korea for a few days, and I may go to China, too. I might go to a conference in Australia, as well.

Language Builder

The future tense

1. Lee and Paula are going to buy a house some time this year.
2. David is playing soccer next Sunday.
3. Michelle will go back to Switzerland after she graduates.

Controlled practice

This summer

1 

2 

3 

He's going to rob a bank.

He's probably going to (will probably) ______________

He may ______________

4 

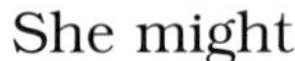

5 

She might ______________

He isn't going to (won't) ______________

Follow-up practice

I hope you can swim

Princess: I wish I could meet a handsome prince! And I wish we could run away to a romantic place far away.

Frog: I'm a handsome prince.

Princess: Ooh! May I kiss you?

Frog: Sure.

Princess: I hope you're going to be very handsome.

KISS

... But you aren't changing.

Frog: Me! I'm not going to change! You're going to become a frog. Don't worry! We can hop over to that pond over there. It's not far, but it's very romantic. I hope you can swim.

Pair practice

The students make sentences about themselves using the patterns "I think ..." and "I hope ...". It's probably best to state the number of sentences the students should make using each pattern.

A. Gradual pictures
I think it's going to be a car.
B. Future trips
I'm going to Austria next month.
probably
may
might
What are you going to do there ?
I'll probably go hiking.
I may swim in the Danube...
C. Fortune telling
Photocopiable
You're going to have five children.
going to
probably
may
might
won't

2 Consolidation Exercises

1. Your future

a. I'll probably ____________________ five years from now.

b. I may ____________________ ten years from now.

c. I won't ____________________ fifteen years from now.

d. I might ____________________ twenty years from now.

2. What do you think will happen next year?

a. ____________________

b. ____________________

3. Hope

a. *She hopes it isn't going to rain.*

b. ____________________

c. ____________________

4. Wish

a. ____________________

b. ____________________

c. ____________________

Questionnaire

What do you hope will happen?

What do you wish?

Too • Enough 3

Lead-in

It's too expensive

Paula: We'd like to buy a house.

Agent: How about this one? It has a large living room and six bedrooms. It's only $1,000,000.

Paula: It's too big and too expensive!

Agent: Well, how about this one? It's $80,000.

Paula: That's too cheap! What's wrong with it?

Agent: It's haunted.

Lee: Haunted!

Agent: Don't worry too much. The ghosts are very friendly.

Emel: You're a fantastic tennis player! You could be a professional.

Carmen: I don't think so. My backhand isn't good enough, and my serve isn't powerful enough.

Emel: You don't practice enough. You should play more often.

Carmen: I'm too busy. I have to work and do all the housework, too.

Emel: Manuel doesn't help you enough.

Carmen: I know!

Language Builder

Too/enough with adjectives

Marc's rock band is too loud.

Emel's bike isn't (bike's not) fast enough.

Too/enough with verbs

Carmen's dog eats too much

Kim doesn't sleep enough

Controlled practice

Too much / enough

1 

He sleeps too much.

2 

He doesn't sleep enough.

3 

4 

5 

6 

Follow-up practice

How about some golf clubs?

Mrs. Shakespeare:	I'm looking for a present for my husband.
Clerk:	How about some golf clubs?
Mrs. Shakespeare:	No, he's too lazy to play golf.
Clerk:	Why not buy him a jacket?
Mrs. Shakespeare:	No, it isn't cold enough yet.
Clerk:	Why don't you give him a word processor? Maybe he could write a detective story.
Mrs. Shakespeare:	That's a good idea. But, word processors are too expensive. Do you have a notebook and some pencils?
Clerk:	Sure. Do you want 2B or HB?
Mrs. Shakespeare:	Let me think. 2B or not 2B?
Clerk:	That's a good line. He should put it in his detective story.

Pair practice

Student A: a clerk in a general store. Student B: him/herself or a famous person.
Student B is looking for a present. Student A makes suggestions which Student B generally refuses. Student B should always give a reason for refusing, using "... too ..." or "... enough ...".

A. Identical pictures

B. Tennis

C. Haunted castle

Photocopiable

3 Consolidation Exercises

1. Too / Enough

a. It's too big.
It isn't small enough.

b. ______

c. ______

2. Your family and friends

Name ______
He/She's too ______ .
He/She isn't ______ enough.
He/She ______ too much.
He/She doesn't ______ enough.

Name ______
He/She's too ______ .
He/She isn't ______ enough.
He/She ______ too much.
He/She doesn't ______ enough.

3. Four Patterns

a. Why can't you climb Mount Everest?
It's too ______
It ______ enough.
I'm too ______
I'm ______ enough.

b. Why can't you buy a new Rolls Royce?
They're too ______
They ______ enough.
I'm too ______
I'm ______ enough.

c. Why can't you touch the ceiling?
It's too ______
It ______ enough.
I'm too ______
I'm ______ enough.

Questionnaire

What do you do too much?

What don't you do enough?

What job/subject do you think ...

a. is too difficult?

b. isn't interesting enough?

c. is too dangerous?

d. isn't challenging enough?

Verb + ing • Verb + to 4

Lead-in But you love windsurfing!

Sachiko is fed up with windsurfing. She hates lifting up the heavy sail and falling in the water all the time. She wants to try parasailing instead. David doesn't want to give up windsurfing. He's just getting used to balancing and controlling the sail. He wants Sachiko to go parasailing by herself.

Sachiko: Please, come parasailing with me!

David: Why don't you go by yourself. I want to learn to windsurf.

Sachiko: Don't you want to be with me?

David: Of course I do. But we don't need to be together all the time. It's nice to have different interests.

Sachiko: Are you trying to leave me?

David: Of course not. ... Oh, OK. Let's go parasailing together. I didn't mean to upset you.

Sachiko: I don't feel like parasailing anymore!

Language Builder

Manuel would like to change his job.

Lee and Paula are trying to find a house.

Michelle is fed up with doing housework.

Sunee's getting used to speaking English every day.

Controlled practice to + ing / to + i~~ng~~

1 

He forgot to telephone his wife.

2 

He's getting used to ______

3 

He's trying to ______

4 

He's looking forward to ______

5 

He's learning to ______

Follow-up practice I'm fed up with eating flies!

Princess: I hate being a frog! I want to be a princess again.

Frog: Why?

Princess: I miss watching TV! I miss going to discos! I miss playing sports!

Frog: But we play a lot of sports! We do the long jump, the high jump ...

Princess: ... And I'm fed up with eating flies! We have flies for breakfast, flies for lunch, flies for dinner ...

Frog: Maybe we should change the menu. The flies don't like it either.

Princess: I can't stand living in this pond! Change me back into a princess!

Frog: OK. But, can I come and visit you sometimes?

Princess: Sure. But don't forget to wipe your feet before entering the palace.

Pair practice

The students make sentences about themselves using the board prompts "I hate ...", "I'm fed up with ..." "I miss ...", "I can't stand ...", and other similar patterns which the teacher may want to introduce.

A. Adding sentences

B. Telepathy

C. Questionnaire

Photocopiable

4 Consolidation Exercises

1. Getting used to

a. Last year she hated getting up early, but now she's getting used to it.

b. Last year ______ a big city, ______

c. Last year ______

2. Feel like

a. She feels like going swimming (going for a swim).

b. ______

c. ______

3. Your family and friends

a. ______ is fed up with ______

b. ______ misses ______

c. ______ can't stand ______

d. ______ often forgets to ______

e. ______ is learning to ______

f. ______ wants to give up ______

Questionnaire

What are you fed up with?

What do you often forget to do?

What are you getting used to?

What do you feel like doing?

Opinions and beliefs

Lead-in What's your job like?

Manuel: What's your job like?

Kim: It's not bad. The pay's good, and there are a lot of chances to travel. But, I have to do a lot of overtime.

Manuel: What's your boss like?

Kim: She's easy to work with and I think she trusts me. But she always worries about money.

David: What do you think of your English lessons?

Sunee: I like them a lot, but I'd like more chances to talk about the world.

David: What do you mean?

Sunee: I'd like to talk about things like the greenhouse effect, third world problems, and deforestation.

David: But, subjects like that are very difficult.

Sunee: I know they're difficult, but they're more interesting than subjects like windsurfing or buying a house. They're much more important, too.

Language Builder

1. What kind of movies do you like?
2. What's San Francisco like?
3. What do you think of big cities like Tokyo?
4. What does your boss look like?

Controlled practice

What do they believe in?

1

Sachiko believes in the Loch Ness Monster.

2

Marc ______________________

3

Michelle ______________________

4

Sunee ______________________

5

Manuel ______________________

Follow-up practice

Do you believe in humans?

Glug: Do you believe in humans?

Zork: You mean strange aliens with two arms and two legs.

Glug: Yes, that's right.

Zork: No, of course not.

Glug: Well, I do. And I think they're intelligent.

Zork: Where do you think they live?

Glug: On Earth!

Zork: On Earth! Ho! Ho! Ho! That's impossible. It's much too polluted!

Glug: Yes, but where does the pollution come from?

Zork: That's a mystery. But it certainly doesn't come from *intelligent* humans.

Pair practice

The students use the ideas in the dialogue as a basis for asking each other whether they believe in UFOs, ghosts, the Loch Ness Monster, etc. (prompts can be put on the board). They should be encouraged to have simple discussions.

A. Broken telephone

B. Debating

C. Computer dating

5 Consolidation Exercises

1. Worries about

a. He worries about money.

b.

What do you worry about?

1.

2.

3.

2. More chances

a. He'd like more chances to meet people.

b.

What would you like more chances to do?

1.

2.

3.

Questionnaire

What's your job/school like?

What's your boss/teacher like?

What do you think of your English lessons?

What subjects would you like to talk about in your English lessons?

What do you think of smoking?

What do you think of school uniforms?

What do you think of your country's government?

Describing places 6

Lead-in What's Chiang Mai like?

Michelle: Where are you from?

Sunee: I'm from Chiang Mai in Thailand.

Sachiko: I fly to Bangkok sometimes, but I don't know the rest of Thailand. What's Chiang Mai like?

Sunee: It's an old city about seven hundred kilometers northwest of Bangkok. The people are very friendly and the stores and restaurants are very good. And it has about three hundred temples! Next time you fly to Thailand you should go there. I'm sure you'll like it.

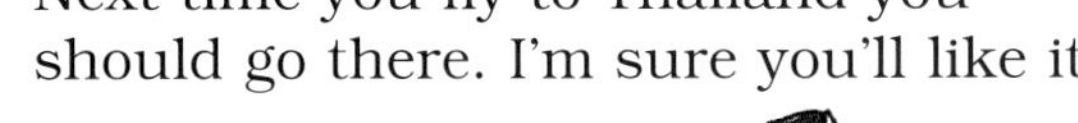

Michelle: What do you do?

Sunee: I have my own importing business.

Sachiko: Do you travel a lot?

Sunee Yes, I import a lot of goods from India, so I go to Calcutta a few times a year.

Sachiko: What's Calcutta like?

Sunee: It's a very interesting city. But there are too many people and there's too much pollution.

Michelle: Are there a lot of social problems?

Sunee: Yes, there aren't enough houses and there isn't enough work.

Language Builder

There are too many cars in Rome.

There's too much crime in Washington.

There aren't enough parking spaces in Tokyo.

There isn't enough (There's not enough) sunshine in London.

Controlled practice

In big cities

1. There's too much pollution.
2. ______________________ parks.
3. ______________________ people.
4. ______________________ green.
5. ______________________ traffic.
6. ______________________ fresh air.
7. ______________________ tall buildings.
8. ______________________ places for children to play.

There are too many
There aren't enough

There's too much
There isn't enough

Follow-up practice

May I ask you some questions?

Man: May I ask you some questions?
Princess: Sure.
Man: Do you live in a house or an apartment?
Princess: In a house.
Man: And what's your neighborhood like?
Princess: It's very nice. There's a large park with deer in it just around the corner.
Man: Are there any fast food restaurants?
Princess: I don't know. I usually eat at home.
Man: And who do you live with?
Princess: My father, my mother, and about fifty frogs!

Pair practice

Student A: a person doing a survey. Student B: him/herself or a famous person.
Student A asks the questions in the dialogue and other similar questions which he/she knows or can guess how to say. Student B gives true answers or plays the role of a famous person.

A. What place is it?

B. Tour guides

C. Challenge

Photocopiable

6 Consolidation Exercises

1. Four patterns

In your town/city

There are too many ______________________

There aren't enough ______________________

There's too much ______________________

There isn't enough ______________________

In your country

There are too many ______________________

There aren't enough ______________________

There's too much ______________________

There isn't enough ______________________

In the world

There are too many ______________________

There aren't enough ______________________

There's too much ______________________

There isn't enough ______________________

2. Quiz

Where's Beijing?

It's in the northeast of China.

Where's Sydney?

Where's Los Angeles?

Where's New Delhi?

Questionnaire

Where do you live?

Do you live in a house or apartment?

What's your house/apartment like?

How many people do you live with?

What's your neighborhood like?

What's your town/city like?

Where else would you like to live? Why?

Past continuous

Lead-in Last night at eleven o'clock

Kim was working in his office. He was writing an important report, but he was very tired so he was falling asleep. He was drinking a lot of coffee to stay awake.

Marc was playing in a rock concert. His fans were going crazy. They were shouting and screaming, and some of them were climbing onto the stage to touch him.

Carmen was waiting for Manuel. She was sitting in a chair and dreaming of being a famous tennis player. She was eating a lot to try and forget that she was lonely.

Language Builder

Sachiko plays the drums.

She played the drums from six o'clock to eight o'clock.

She was playing the drums at seven o'clock.

Controlled practice At ten o'clock

1

She was having breakfast.

2

3

4

5

6

Follow-up practice The dog was tired

Romeo: What were you doing at three o'clock yesterday afternoon?

Juliet: I can't remember.

Romeo: I saw you! You were walking in the park with Bruce!

Juliet: I was taking the dog for a walk.

Romeo: You were holding Bruce's hand!

Juliet: He was taking the dog for a walk, too.

Romeo: Then, you got into Bruce's Cadillac.

Juliet: The dog was tired.

Romeo: And you got home at two o'clock in the morning!

Juliet: The dog was hungry, so we took him out for dinner.

Pair practice

Student A asks Student B what he/she was doing at a particular time, and should be suspicious about his/her answers. Student B gives true answers or plays the role of a famous person.

A. Witnesses

B. Last sentence

C. What was happening?

Photocopiable

7 Consolidation Exercises

1. Why do people take vacations?

a. to *go sightseeing*
b. to *relax on the beach*
c. to
d. to

2. Why do people work/study?

a. to
b. to
c. to
d. to

3. Why do people learn foreign languages?

a. to
b. to
c. to
d. to

4. What were they doing at three o'clock ?

a.

b.

c.

d.

e.

Questionnaire

Where were you at nine o'clock last night?

What were you doing?

Where were you at ten o'clock yesterday morning?

What were you doing?

Where do you think you were at three o'clock in the afternoon on August 21st last year?

What do you think you were doing?

Comparatives 8

Lead-in: It isn't as exciting as the city

David: It's wonderful to get away from the city! I wish I could live here! It's so much quieter and more peaceful than the city.

Sachiko: But there aren't any stores! And there aren't any nightclubs!

David: I know the countryside isn't as exciting as the city, and I know it isn't as convenient. But it's so much more relaxing here. It's much cleaner, too.

Sachiko: It isn't cleaner! Look at my new shoes. They're covered in mud!

Dear Paula,

David and I are spending the weekend in Wisconsin.

The countryside around here is almost as beautiful as the Japan Alps. But, it's as boring as Tokyo on New Year's Day! There's nothing to do!

See you soon.

With love from,

Sachiko

Language Builder

Manuel's lazier than Carmen.

Michelle's more intelligent than Marc.

Lee isn't (Lee's not) as busy as Kim.

Sunee is as quiet as a mouse.

Controlled practice as ... as

1. Oxford ______________ modern ______________
2. Oxford ______________ busy ______________
3. Oxford doesn't have ______________ many tall buildings ______________
4. Oxford doesn't have ______________ traffic ______________

Follow-up practice Do you miss me?

Romeo: Do you miss me sometimes?
Juliet: Yes, of course.
Romeo: Do you miss me every night?
Juliet: No, not as much as that.
Romeo: Once a week?
Juliet: No, more than that.
Romeo: Three or four times a week?
Juliet: Yes, that's about right. The balcony's quite high, and it's difficult to see in the dark.

Pair practice

Student A asks Student B questions using the pattern "Do you sometimes ...?". When answers are "Yes", Student A tries to find out how often Student B does these things. Student B answers "No, more than that", "No, not as much as that", or "Yes, that's about right".

A. What is it?

B. Pairs

C. Word Derby

Photocopiable

8 Consolidation Exercises

1. not as

a. 

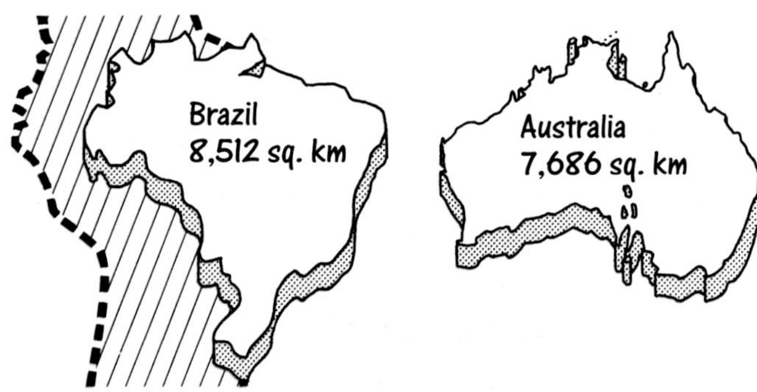

b. ______________________

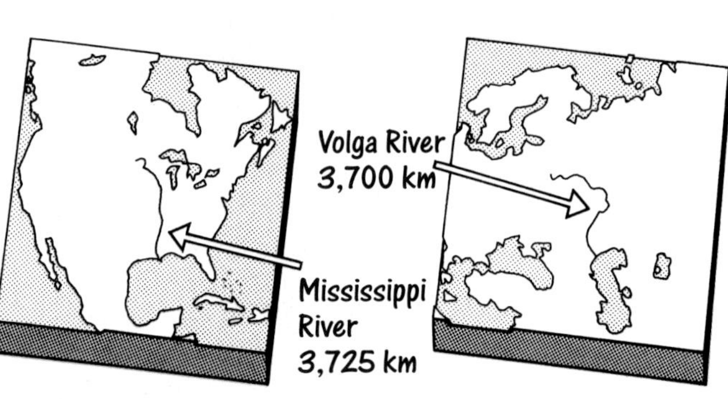

c. ______________________

Atlantic Ocean 5,608 m

Pacific Ocean 11,022 m

d. ______________________

2. No, not as much as that. / No, more than that. / Yes, that's about right.

Do you sleep six hours a night?

____

Do you speak English every day?

____

Do you take a vacation once every two years?

____

Do you go to the movies once a month?

____

Do you go swimming three times a year?

____

Do you fall in love once every two weeks?

____

Questionnaire

Use ... *isn't as* ... or ... *aren't as* ...

Which do you think is more interesting, baseball or soccer?

____

Which do you think is more exciting, waterskiing or surfing?

____

Which do you think are more intelligent, dolphins or monkeys?

____

Which do you think are more dangerous, tarantulas or sharks?

____

A. Warmer or colder?

B. Five sentences

C. Concentration

Photocopiable

9 Consolidation Exercises

1. Graphs

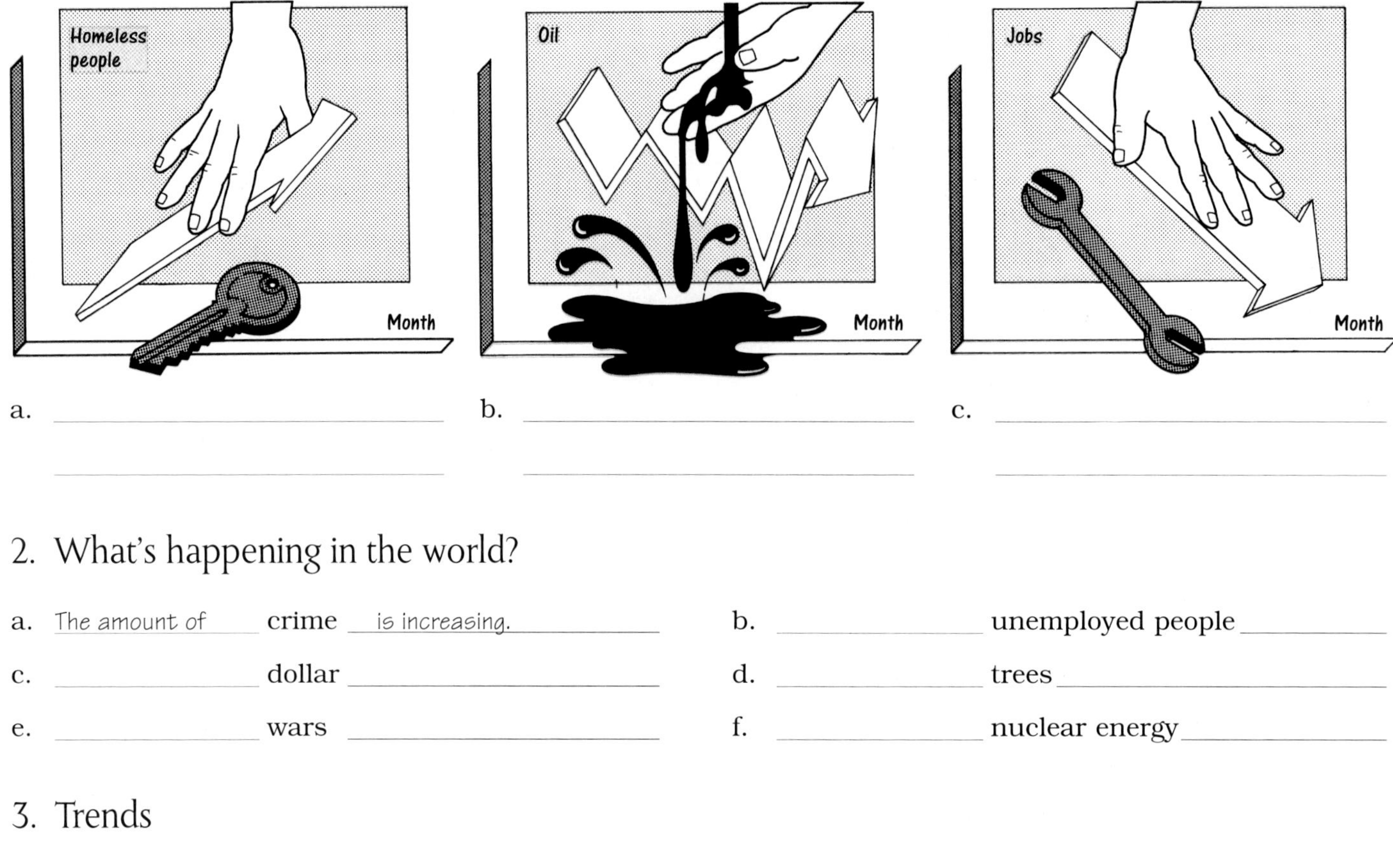

a. ______________________

b. ______________________

c. ______________________

2. What's happening in the world?

a. The amount of crime is increasing.

b. ______ unemployed people ______

c. ______ dollar ______

d. ______ trees ______

e. ______ wars ______

f. ______ nuclear energy ______

3. Trends

What's getting better?

What's getting worse?

What's becoming popular?

What's going out of fashion?

Questionnaire

How do you think your life will change in the future?

1. ______________________
2. ______________________
3. ______________________
4. ______________________

How do you think the world will change in the future?

1. ______________________
2. ______________________
3. ______________________
4. ______________________

Superlatives 10

Lead-in

I'm the best guitarist in France!

Marc: I'm the best guitarist in France! My concerts are always sold out, and my albums are always at the top of the charts.

Carmen: Are you very rich?

Marc: Yes, I'm the richest rock star in France.

Manuel: So, why are you learning English with us?

Marc: I can't go to an English school in Paris. Everybody knows me. I'm the most popular superstar in Paris.

Carmen: I wish I could live in Paris!

Marc: I don't always live there. I also have houses in Rome, London, Tokyo, and New York.

Carmen: Which do you like best?

Marc: Oh, Paris! It's the most exciting city in the world. It has the best nightclubs, the best concerts, the most exciting new fashions ...

Manuel: I went there once. It rained all the time! And I listened to one of your albums last week. It was awful!

Language Builder

Manuel's the tallest student in the class.

Michelle's probably the most intelligent student in the class.

Carmen's the best tennis player in the class.

Marc's probably the worst baseball player in the class.

Controlled practice — Geography

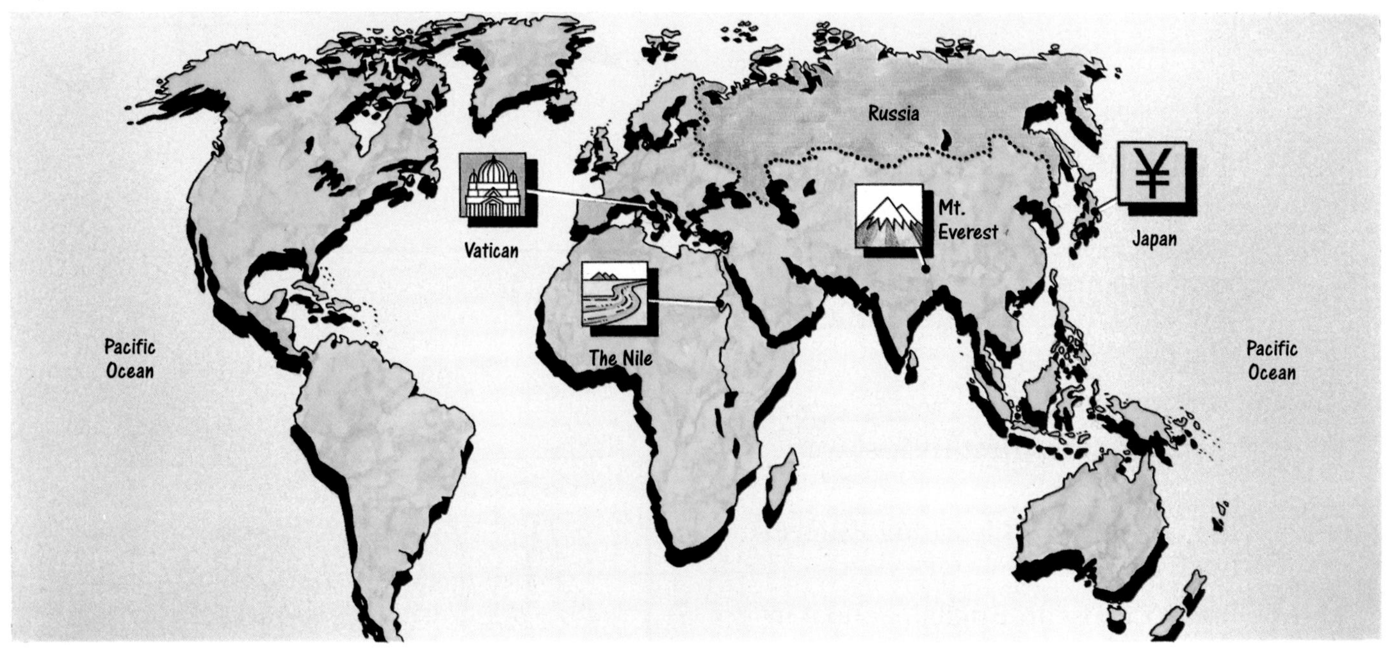

1 Mount Everest is the highest mountain in the world.

2 __________ deepest __________

3 __________ longest __________

4 __________ smallest __________

5 __________ most expensive __________

6 __________ largest __________

Follow-up practice — I don't agree

Boris: Who do you think's the most intelligent person in the cave?

Frank: I've an …

Boris: Yes, I agree. Ivan invented fire. He's the most intelligent. Who do you think's the best hunter in the cave?

Frank: I've an …

Boris: Ivan! I don't agree. He can't hit a mammoth from two meters!

Frank: I've an idea.

Boris: What?

Frank: Let's use the car.

Pair practice

The students take turns to ask each other questions using the patterns "Who do you think's the best/most … in the class/office/school/city/country/world, etc."

A. Hands

B. Sets of three

C. Quiz

Photocopiable

10 Consolidation Exercises

1. In your country

Who do you think's the best actor/actress?

______

Who do you think's the most popular singer?

______

Which city do you think's the most polluted?

______

Which area do you think's the nicest?

______

2. -est / most

The ants are the smallest.

______

______

______

______

______

______

______

______

______

______

______

3. U.S.A. Quiz

a. The Mississippi is the longest river in the U.S.A.

b. New York is ______

c. Mount McKinley is ______

d. Alaska is ______

e. ______

Questionnaire

What's the newest thing you have?

A computer.

What's the largest thing you have?

______

What's the oldest thing you have?

______

What's the most dangerous thing you have?

______

What's the noisiest thing you have?

______

What's the most beautiful thing you have?

______

Present perfect •1• 11

Lead-in I've seen it three times

Marc: We're going to the new Spielberg movie. Do you want to come with us?

Sachiko: No thanks. I've seen it three times.

Marc: Well, why don't you come for a drive with us? I have a great car.

Sachiko: I know. I've been in it about ten times before.

Marc: Well, how about having dinner with us later? Have you been to the new Mexican restaurant near the station?

Sachiko: Yes, I've been there twice with David.

Language Builder

Sachiko has traveled all over the world.

Paula has painted a lot of beautiful pictures.

David has played soccer in Brazil.

Marc has met a lot of famous people.

Kim has written a popular book.

Carmen has seen a UFO.

Controlled practice — What have they done?

1

Sachiko has been to Australia.

2

Manuel ____________________

3

Carmen ____________________

4

Kim ____________________

5

Michelle ____________________

6

David ____________________

Follow-up practice — Have you ever broken a bone?

Juliet:	That looks very dangerous! Have you ever hurt your hand?
Bruce:	Yes, many times.
Juliet:	Have you ever broken a bone?
Bruce:	Oh yes. I've broken my brother's arm, my English teacher's leg ...
Juliet:	I mean, have you ever broken the bones in your own hands or feet?
Bruce:	Yes, I've broken my hands and feet in a lot of places.
Juliet:	Karate sounds very dangerous!
Bruce:	Yes, but I'm more careful now. I don't go to those places.

Pair practice

The students take turns to ask "Have you ever ...?" questions (e.g. "Have you ever broken your leg?", "Have you ever been to New York?"). They should be encouraged to ask natural follow-up questions.

A. Crossword

B. Have you ever?

C. Concentration

Photocopiable

11 Consolidation Exercises

1. What have they done?

a. 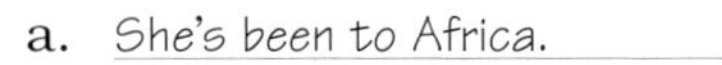 She's been to Africa.

b. ______

c. ______

d. ______

e. ______

f. ______

2. She's been to / She hasn't been to ... yet

a. She's been to Tokyo.

b. ______

c. ______

d. ______

e. ______

f. ______

Questionnaire

I've been ______

I've seen ______

I've met ______

I've eaten ______

I've broken ______

I've played ______

I've won ______

I've ______

I've ______

I've ______

Present perfect •2•

Lead-in We've been to a party

Patrolman: Could I see your driver's licence, please?

Marc: Sure, here you are.

Patrolman: So, you're French.

Marc: Yes, that's right.

Patrolman: Have you been here long?

Marc: About two or three months.

Patrolman: And what have you been doing this evening?

Marc: We've been to a party.

Patrolman: Have you been drinking?

Marc: Only orange juice.

Patrolman: And why were you speeding?

Marc: I wasn't speeding!

Patrolman: Yes, you were! You were driving at ninety miles per hour.

Marc: How do you know?

Patrolman: I checked my speedometer.

Marc: So you were speeding, too.

Language Builder

Emel has lived/has been living in Ankara for three years, and she's going to live there for one more year.

David has taught/has been teaching for three hours, but now he's taking a break.

Controlled practice

What have they been doing?

1

Kim has been working hard/has worked hard all day, and now he's watching TV.

2

Michelle has been studying hard/has studied computer science for two years, and she's going to study for another two years.

3

Carmen ____________/____________ two hours, ______________________________

4

Emel ____________/____________ economics _____ three years ______________ year.

Follow-up practice

What have you been doing recently?

Boris:	Hello, Nessie! What have you been doing recently?
Nessie:	I've been lying at the bottom of this lake.
Boris:	How long have you been here?
Nessie:	For a few thousand years. Since just after the last Ice Age.
Boris:	Why have you been here so long?
Nessie:	I've tried to leave, but somebody always tries to take my photograph.
Boris:	You shouldn't be so shy!

Pair practice

Student A asks Student B the question "What have you been doing recently?" followed by "How long have you been ...?", or "How long did you ...?" if the action has finished. The students then develop the conversation. Student B gives true answers or plays the role of a famous person.

A. Leaving the room
Have you moved this chair?
B. How long have I had ...?
How long have I had my watch?
I think you've had it for three years.
C. What has happened?
Photocopiable
Thank you!
Has somebody given you a present?
Has somebody helped you?
Thank you!

12 Consolidation Exercises

1. What has happened?

a. She's woken up.

b. ______________________

c. ______________________

2. For / Since

a. He's been living here for five years.

______________ since ______________

b. She started reading that book three days ago.

______________ for ______________

c. She's been playing tennis since ten o'clock this morning. It's now three o'clock in the afternoon.

______________ for ______________

d. He's been doing the same job for ten years, but today he was fired.

______________ since ______________

Questionnaire

What have you been doing recently?

____

What has happened at work/school recently?

____

How long have you worked/studied today?

____

What has happened in your town/city recently?

____

Where have you been recently?

____

What has happened in your country recently?

____

How long have you been learning English?

____

What has happened in the world recently?

____

Present perfect •3•

Lead-in I've just come back from ...

Sunee: Hello, Kim. How have you been?

Kim: Pretty good. I've been visiting some relatives in Korea for a few days. I flew to Cheju Island on Friday, and I came back last night.

Sunee: I've been to Korea a couple of times. In fact, I visited Seoul earlier this year. But I haven't been to Cheju Island. I've heard it's a very nice place.

Kim: I think it's one of the most beautiful islands in the world.

Kim: Cheju's changed a lot since I was a child. These days there are a lot more foreign tourists, especially from Japan, and some areas have become very commercialized.

Sunee: Is that a big problem?

Kim: Not really. It's been very good for the local economy, and most of the island is still unspoiled. Some of the local customs have been disappearing, of course. But that's happening all over the world.

Language Builder

Present perfect – past simple

Emel has been to Florida.
Michelle went to Florida last year

Carmen has been playing a lot of tennis.
David played soccer on Sunday

Changes

1 

The town has become commercialized.

2 

3 

4 

polluted ~~commercialized~~ unsafe crowded

I've never flown in a plane before

Boris: I've never flown in a plane before.

Bruce: Have you ever flown without a plane?

Boris: I tried making some wings once, but they didn't work.
... Wow! Look down there! I've never seen such small people! They look like ants!

Bruce: They are ants. We haven't taken off yet.

Boris: We haven't taken off! But I'm already feeling nervous! In fact, I've never felt so nervous in my life! ... Um ... Do planes crash very often?

Bruce: No, only once.

Pair practice

The students make sentences about themselves using the pattern ("I've never ..."). It's probably best to state the number of sentences they should make. The student who is listening should be encouraged to ask natural follow-up questions.

A. Adding sentences

B. Challenge

C. Mime

Photocopiable

13 Consolidation Exercises

1. Yes, I have / No, I haven't

Have you ever seen a kangaroo?

Have you ever met a famous person?

Have you ever played rugby?

Have you ever eaten tacos?

Have you ever written a poem?

Have you ever ridden a motorcycle?

2. Never

I've never ______

I've never ______

I've never ______

I've never ______

3. Present perfect or past simple?

a. I studied English very hard yesterday.

b. I ______ been ______

c. I have ______ seen ______

d. I ______ two years ago.

e. I ______ last week.

f. I ______ eaten ______

Questionnaire

Where were you born? ______

What's your home/town city like? ______

How has your home/town city changed since you were a child?

How has your country changed since you were a child?

How has the world changed since you were a child?

How have you changed since you were a child?

Reported speech •1• 14

Lead-in

You said it had a fantastic view!

Agent:	Here we are. Your dream home! Isn't it wonderful?
Lee:	But, you said it had a beautiful yard!
Agent:	Well, it will have after you plant some flowers.
Paula:	And you said it had a fantastic view!
Agent:	Don't you like tall apartment buildings? I think they're fascinating.
Lee:	And you said we would love the modern design. It looks about a hundred years old!
Agent:	It's only sixty years old. And it's very cheap! It's only $200,000!
Paula:	$200,000! You said it was $80,000!
Agent:	Well, OK. I'm feeling very generous today. You can have it for $150,000.

Language Builder

Carmen said "I'm busy." = Carmen said she was/is busy.

Lee said "I'll call her." = Lee said he would/will call her.

Emel said "I ran home." = Emel said she had run/ran home.

Kim said "I've finished." = Kim said he had/has finished.

Controlled practice What did they say?

1

He said he liked fishing.
He said he likes fishing.

2

3

4

5

6

Follow-up practice There is life on Earth!

Glug: There is life on Earth! I've found three different aliens!

Zork: Are they intelligent?

Glug: I'll ask them some questions. What's 12 ÷ 3 x 2 – 7.5?

Seal: Aarf!

Glug: The seal said 12 ÷ 3 x 2 – 7.5 is a half.

Zork: That was quick! Ask the frog a question.

Glug: Have you read *The Complete Works of Shakespeare*?

Frog: Redit!

Glug: The frog said he has read *The Complete Works of Shakespeare*.

Zork: That's very good! Ask the dog a question.

Glug: Which German composer was born in 1685?

Dog: Bark!

Glug: The dog said that Bach was born in 1685.

Zork: They're all very intelligent!

Groups of three practice

Student A: a reporter. Student B: him/herself or a famous person. Student C: an editor.
Student A interviews Student B and reports each answer to Student C. Student B gives true answers or plays the role of a famous person.

A. Mixed sentences

B. Reporting an interview

C. Long sentences

Photocopiable

14 Consolidation Exercises

1. He/She said?

a. He said he loves her.
He said he loved her.

b. ______

c. ______

d. ______

e. ______

f. ______

2. What did they say?

a. Carmen said she didn't want to go fishing.
Carmen: I don't want to go fishing.

b. Manuel said Marc couldn't sing well.
Manuel: ______

c. Paula said she was going to paint a picture.
Paula: ______

d. Kim said he wouldn't go to Seattle.
Kim: ______

Questionnaire

What have people said to you?

My mother said I would never be rich.

a. ______

b. ______

c. ______

d. ______

Interested • Interesting 15

Lead-in It's so frustrating

Lee: I'm tired of looking for a house.

Paula: Yes, it's very tiring!

Lee: It's so frustrating!

Paula: Yes, I'm frustrated, too. Why don't we buy the haunted house? It's very cheap, and we can fix it up.

Lee: How about the ghosts?

Paula: I'm not frightened of ghosts! I don't believe in them.

Sachiko: What's the matter, David?

David: Nothing much. I'm just a bit depressed. That's all.

Sachiko: Why?

David: I'm not satisfied with my teaching.

Sachiko: That's silly. Your classes are great! They're really exciting!

David: Paula and Emel don't think so. They're disappointed because their English isn't getting better.

Language Builder

Michelle thinks exams are depressing.
Exams make Michelle (feel) depressed.

Kim thinks long meetings are tiring.
Long meetings make Kim (feel) tired.

Controlled practice

How are they feeling?

1 

He's satisfied.

2 

____

3 

____

4 

____

5

____

depressed   ~~satisfied~~   frightened   frustrated   disappointed

Follow-up practice

You look tired

Bruce: You look tired.

Romeo: I've been chasing Juliet.

Bruce: Why does that make you tired?

Romeo: She runs very fast.

Bruce: You look depressed, too.

Romeo: Juliet doesn't love me. It's terrible! I can't sleep at night.

Bruce: You should see a doctor.

Romeo: I went last week. The doctor said I should drink hot lemon juice after a hot bath every night before I go to bed.

Bruce: Does it work?

Romeo: I don't know. I never finish drinking the hot bath.

Pair practice

Student A starts by saying "You look ...", and Student B answers "I've been ..." (put these patterns on the board as prompts). The students then develop the conversation.

A. Guessing letters

B. Cards

C. Questionnaire (Units 1–15)

Photocopiable

15 Consolidation Exercises

1. I think

I think ______________________ frightening.

______________________ expensive.

______________________ exciting.

______________________ beautiful.

______________________ boring.

______________________ tiring.

______________________ difficult.

______________________ interesting.

______________________ challenging.

______________________ noisy.

2. Make(s) me

______________________ tired.

______________________ frustrated.

______________________ angry.

______________________ depressed.

______________________ hungry.

______________________ worried.

______________________ happy.

______________________ excited.

______________________ disappointed.

______________________ bored.

3. I've ...

You look tired.

I've just been running.

You look frightened.

____

You look satisfied.

____

You look depressed.

____

You look embarrassed.

____

You look disappointed.

____

You look worried.

____

You look bored.

____

Questionnaire

What world problem are you most worried about?

____

____

What subjects are you most interested in?

____

____

What kind of movies make you most frightened?

____

____

What social problems make you depressed?

____

____

Used to 16

Lead-in We used to be so happy

Manuel: We used to be so happy together. What went wrong?

Carmen: You used to help me! You used to cook dinner! You used to wash the dishes! You used to do the gardening! But, now you don't help me at all!

Manuel: I used to have a lot of spare time. These days I'm too busy!

Carmen: I'm busy, too! I have to work as well, you know!

Manuel: But, you get home earlier than me!

Carmen: Only because you go out drinking! You used to come home straight after work!

Manuel: I have to go drinking. It's part of my work.

Carmen: Yes, but not every night!

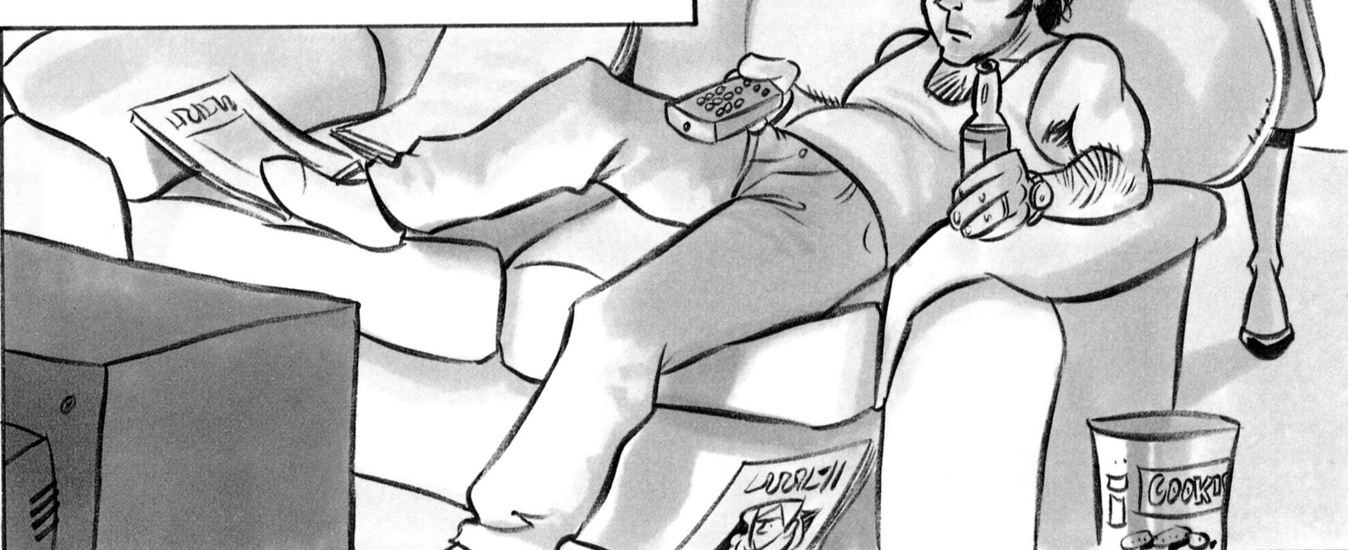

Language Builder

Kim used to play in an orchestra.

Michelle didn't use to study hard.

Did Sachiko use to live in Sapporo? Yes, she did.

Controlled practice Marc used to ...

1 Marc used to stay home in the evenings, but now he goes out every night.

2 ______________ early, ______________ always ______________ late.

3 ______________ school uniform, ______________ usually ______________

Follow-up practice I used to wear a brown belt

Bruce: I'm a black belt!

Juliet: What color belt did you use to wear before the black belt?

Bruce: I used to wear a brown belt.

Juliet: And what color belt did you use to wear before the brown belt?

Bruce: I used to wear a white belt.

Juliet: And what color belt did you use to wear before the white belt?

Bruce: I didn't use to wear a belt. My pants used to fall down.

Pair practice

Student A: an interviewer. Student B: him/herself or a famous person.
Student A asks questions about Student B's present or past situation (e.g. "Who used to be your English teacher?", or "What kind of work do you do?"), and follows up by asking a succession of "... used to ... before that?" questions.

A. True/False

B. Who was he?

C. Time travel

Photocopiable

16 Consolidation Exercises

1. What did they use to be?

a. 

b. ______________________

c. ______________________

d. ______________________

e. ______________________

f. ______________________

2. What did people use to do?

Twenty years ago people used to ______________________

Thirty years ago people used to ______________________

Forty years ago ______________________

One hundred years ago ______________________

One thousand years ago ______________________

Five thousand years ago ______________________

Questionnaire

Ten years ago

What used to be your favorite TV show?

____

What sports team did you use to support?

____

Who used to be your favorite actor/singer?

____

What did you use to like doing on Sundays?

____

Tag questions

Lead-in You're Marc Delon, aren't you?

Judge: You're Marc Delon, aren't you?
Marc: Yes, that's right.
Judge: You live on Bay Street, don't you?
Marc: Yes.
Judge: And you went to a party at your teacher's house on July 25th, didn't you?
Marc: Yes.
Judge: You drank a lot of wine, didn't you?
Marc: Oh, no. I only drank orange juice.
Judge: Your blood test shows that you drank at least three bottles of wine.
Marc: Well, only small bottles.
Judge: You've been to court for speeding twice before, haven't you?
Marc: I can't remember.
Judge: That's twice in three months, isn't it?
Marc: I guess so.
Judge: Well, you'll have to pay $2,000, do fifty hours community service, and stop driving for six months.

Language Builder

Manuel doesn't like dogs, does he?
Sachiko went to Europe last year, didn't she?

Not a real question Paula's an artist, isn't she?
A real question Paula's an artist, isn't she?

Controlled practice

Sachiko's late

1

"Sachiko's late, isn't she?"

2

"She got up ________________, ________________?"

3

"She's missed ________________, ________________?"

4

"She can't ________________, ________________?"

5

"She'll have to ________________, ________________?"

Follow-up practice

You didn't call me, did you?

Frog: You haven't been to see me, have you?

Princess: I've been very busy.

Frog: You didn't call me, did you?

Princess: I wanted to call you, but I lost your number.

Frog: That's a good excuse! There aren't many frogs in the telephone book, are there?

Princess: I'm sorry.

Frog: You aren't really sorry, are you? You just kissed me, had a bit of fun, and then left.

Princess: I'm the first princess you've ever kissed, aren't I?

Frog: No, I've kissed hundreds of princesses before! But, this is the first time I've fallen in love.

Pair practice

Student A is angry with Student B for not doing something (either real or imaginary), and uses tag questions to express his/her anger (e.g. "You were late this morning, weren't you!"). Student B gives excuses. It may be necessary for the teacher to write starting statements on the board.

A. Don't say *Yes* or *No*
You're from Mexico, aren't you?
I'm from Mexico.
B. Alibis
It was raining very hard, wasn't it?
Yes, that's right.
C. Smugglers
Photocopiable
You have diamonds in the suitcase, don't you?
No, I only have dirty clothes.
CUSTOMS

17 Consolidation Exercises

1. Tags

a. He's a lawyer, ___isn't he___?

b. She's playing the piano, ______________?

c. You play baseball, ______________?

d. You didn't see her, ______________?

e. She's been to Canada, ______________?

f. He'll be late, ______________?

g. He won't like it, ______________?

h. I'm your friend, ______________?

2. Who was ...?

Who was Magellan?
He sailed around the world, didn't he?

Who was Abraham Lincoln?
____

Who was Picasso?
____

Who was Ernest Hemingway?
____

Who was Marilyn Monroe?
____

Who was Isaac Newton?
____

3. Sarcasm

He thinks New York is in Australia?
He's extremely intelligent!

He smokes a lot and never plays any sports.
____

She never gives people presents.
____

My home town has a population of only five thousand people.
____

The city baseball team is always at the bottom of the league.
____

His car is slower than a bicycle.
____

Questionnaire

You're learning English, ___aren't you___?
Yes, that's right.

You have green ears, ______________?
____

You'll be sixty next year, ______________?
____

You've been to Paris, ______________?
____

You're Chinese, ______________?
____

You didn't go swimming last week, ______________?
____

You eat a lot of bananas, ______________?
____

You aren't human, ______________?
____

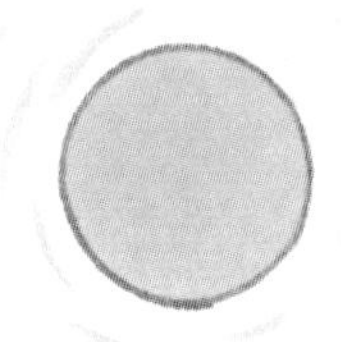

Time clauses • 1 • 18

Lead-in

Congratulate us when we win!

Reporter: Where did you learn to play tennis so well? You're fantastic!

Carmen: I don't know. When I was a child, I played a lot in the local park, but I've never had lessons.

Reporter: You've never had lessons! But you've just beaten last year's champions! How about you, Emel?

Emel: I started playing when I was in high school, and I took part in a few tournaments when I was a teenager. That's all.

Reporter: Well, congratulations!

Carmen: Congratulate us when we win the tournament, not before!

Reporter: When you win! But, some of the best players in the world are taking part.

Carmen: When we win, we're going to have a big party. Why don't you come along?

Language Builder

Sunee studied law when she lived in Bangkok.

When Sunee lived in Bangkok, she studied law.

Same time When Lee was a child he lived in Shanghai.

One after another When Kim goes back to Korea he'll probably get married.

Controlled practice — Michelle's future

1 

She'll probably start working for a software company when she's about twenty-three.

2

____
____________ about twenty-seven.

3 

____
________________ about thirty.

4 

____
____________ about thirty-five.

5

____
________________ about forty.

6 

____
____________ about forty-five.

Follow-up practice — My eye hurts when I drink coffee

Doctor:	What's the matter?
Boris:	My eye hurts when I drink coffee.
Doctor:	Does it hurt when you drink tea?
Boris:	Yes, sometimes.
Doctor:	How about when you drink orange juice?
Boris:	No, it never hurts when I drink orange juice.
Doctor:	Is the pain always in your eye?
Boris:	No, I sometimes get a pain in my nose, but it's usually in my eye.
Doctor:	OK. Take one of these tablets three times a day, and take the spoon out of the coffee before you drink it.

Pair practice

Student A: a doctor. Student B: him/herself or a famous person.
Student B tells Student A about a real or imaginary sickness/injury. Student A tries to find out more and gives advice. The students should be encouraged to use "when" clauses.

A. Newspaper reporters

B. Tennis

C. Mime

Photocopiable

18 Consolidation Exercises

1. Chains

a. When I was a child I watched a lot of TV.
When I watched a lot of TV ____________.
When I ____________.
When ____________.

b. When I'm sixty ____________.
When I ____________.
____________.
____________.

2. What do you think they do when they are bored?

a. ____________

b. ____________

c. ____________

d. ____________

Questionnaire

What do you do ...
when you are tired?
____

when you are angry?
____

when you have a headache?
____

What will you do ...
when you speak English fluently?
____

when you have more money?
____

when you are very old?
____

Time clauses •2• 19

Lead-in When I was a child, I used to ...

Sachiko: How long have you been able to play soccer?

David: Since I was about five. When I was a child, I used to play with my older brother and his friends.

Sachiko: Could you play well?

David: No, I couldn't play well until I was about fifteen.

Sachiko: I've never been able to play a sport well. When I was in high school, I used to play soccer, baseball, and rugby, but I was terrible at all of them.

David: Those are all boys' sports!

Sachiko: Yes, all my friends were boys.

David: You haven't changed.

Sachiko: What do you mean?

Language Builder

Paula used to be a professional artist when she lived in Brazil.

Lee could speak English when he was about six years old.

Marc didn't start playing the guitar until he was seventeen.

Sachiko became a stewardess as soon as she graduated from college.

Controlled practice — A caveman's childhood

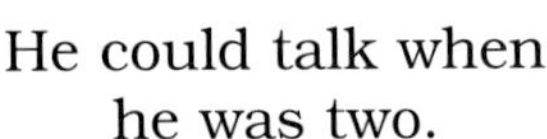
He could talk when he was two.

______________________ four.

______________________ six.

______________________ eight.

______________________ ten.

Follow-up practice — How did you burn your ears?

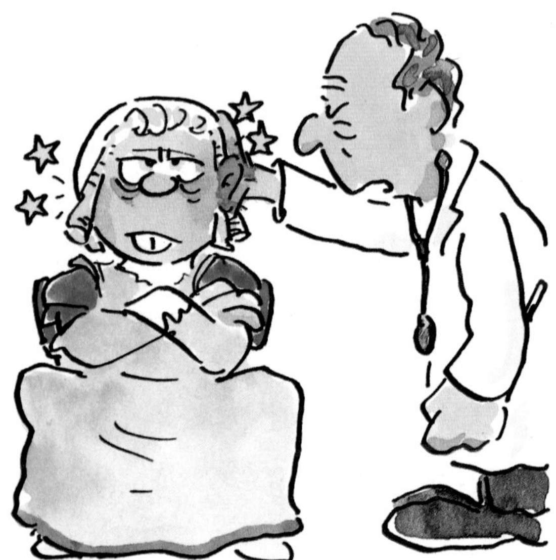

Doctor:	How did you burn your ears?
Mrs. Shakespeare:	The telephone rang when I was doing the ironing.
Doctor:	But why both your ears?
Mrs. Shakespeare:	As soon as I hung up, the telephone rang again.
Doctor:	Well, you'll have to keep these bandages on for about two weeks.
Mrs. Shakespeare:	When my ears are better, will I be able to listen to rock music?
Doctor:	Yes, of course.
Mrs. Shakespeare:	That's wonderful! I never could before. My husband says it disturbs him when he's writing.

Pair practice

Student A: a doctor. Student B: him/herself or a famous person.
This activity is similar to Unit 18, except the teacher writes "when", "able to", "as soon as" (and other words or patterns the students need to practice) on the board.

A. Name an age

One!
used to, couldn't, had to
When I was one, I used to cry a lot. I couldn't walk, I...
B. What do you say?
What do you say when somebody says "Thank you"?
Sachiko's Team 8
Manuel's Team 5
You're welcome.
Any time.
No problem.
C. Snakes and Ladders
Photocopiable
I couldn't ride a bike until I was seven.

19 Consolidation Exercises

1. As soon as

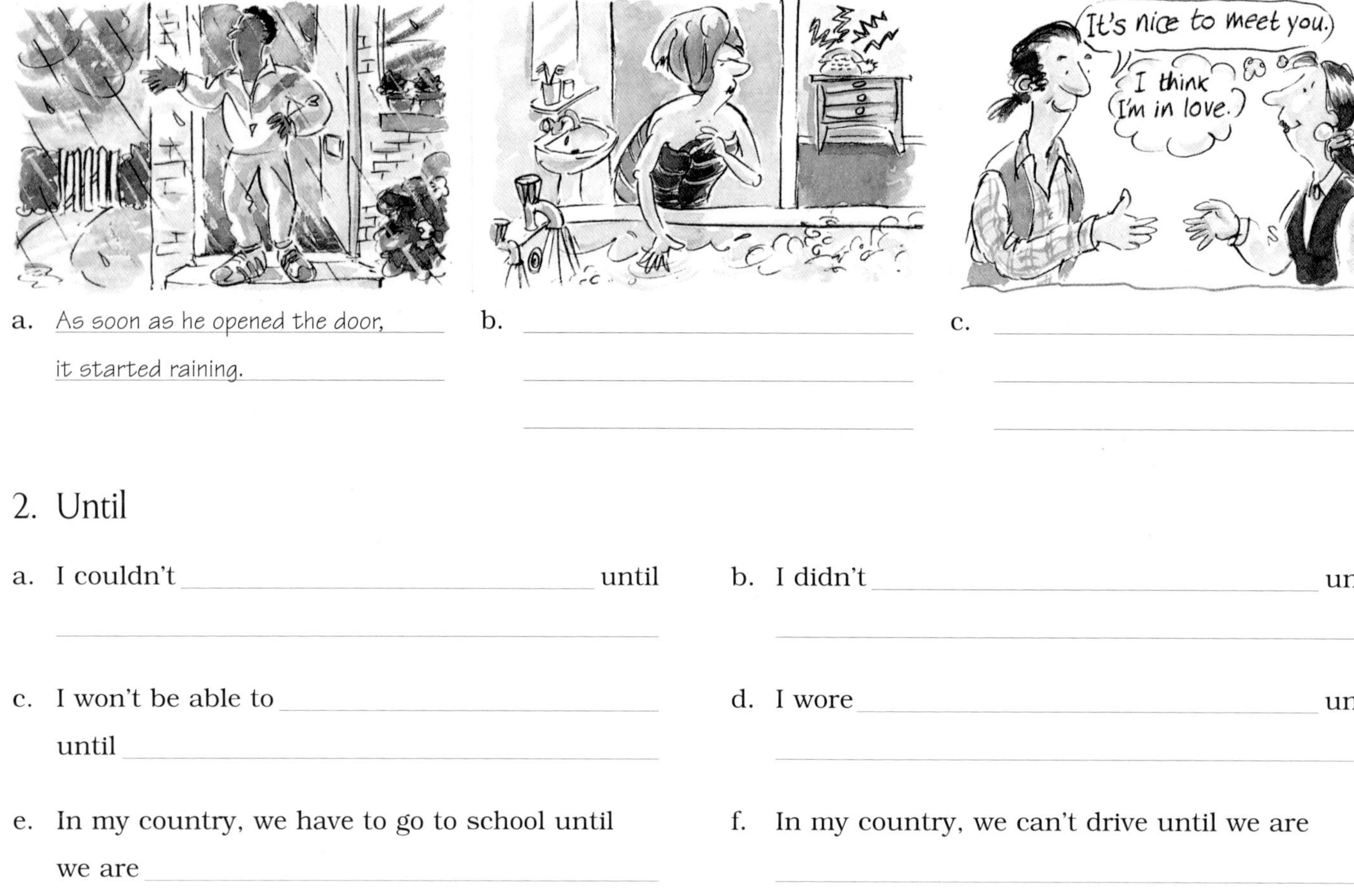

a. *As soon as he opened the door, it started raining.*

b. ______________________

c. ______________________

2. Until

a. I couldn't ______________________ until ______________________

b. I didn't ______________________ until ______________________

c. I won't be able to ______________________ until ______________________

d. I wore ______________________ until ______________________

e. In my country, we have to go to school until we are ______________________

f. In my country, we can't drive until we are ______________________

3. Able to

a. I've been able to ______________________ for ______________________.

b. I've been able to ______________________ since ______________________.

c. I've been able to ______________________ for ______________________.

d. I've been able to ______________________ since ______________________.

Questionnaire

What did you use to do when you were ten?

____

What did you use to do when you were two?

____

As soon as I ______________________, I'm going to ______________________.

I'm not going to ______________________ until ______________________.

I'll be able to ______________________ when ______________________.

I'll have to ______________________ when ______________________.

Noun clauses 20

Lead-in Did you hear what he said?

Carmen: Do you know who that was?

Emel: It was Pete Pampas, the Wimbledon champion, wasn't it? I wonder what he's doing here.

Carmen: Did you hear what he said?

Emel: No, I wasn't listening.

Carmen: He said he knows where we can find a good coach. I think he's going to help us.

Emel: You're kidding!

Michelle: I've been thinking about what Sunee was saying the other day.

Sachiko: You mean about Calcutta.

Michelle: Yes, I've been wondering what we can do to help. There are millions of poor people in the world, but we just lie in the sun and go to parties.

Sachiko: I know what you mean, but we can't do anything to help. And I like lying in the sun and going to parties.

Michelle: Yes, me too. But don't you think it's selfish?

Sachiko: Not really. Everybody likes to have fun.

Michelle: Well, I think we should do something!

Language Builder

know/wonder/remember/understand/believe
+ what/where/when/who/why/which/how ...

Marc can't remember what he did last night.
Emel doesn't understand why Carmen got married.

Controlled practice

A superstar's vacation

1 She's wondering where to go.

2 __________ when __________

3 __________ how __________

4 __________ how __________

5 ______________________

Follow-up practice

He can play poker

Juliet: I've lost my dog.
Policeman: Do you know where you lost him?
Juliet: He ran away in the park.
Policeman: Do you know how we can recognize him?
Juliet: He's small with curly, light-brown hair, and he can play poker.
Policeman: He can play poker!
Juliet: Yes, but he isn't very good. He always wags his tail when he gets good cards.
Policeman: Do you know why he ran away?
Juliet: I think he saw a UFO.
Policeman: Well, nobody has found him.
Juliet: Do you know what I can do?
Policeman: You could put an ad in the newspaper.
Juliet: But he can't read!

Pair practice

Student A: a police officer. Student B: somebody who has lost something.
Student B reports losing something. Student A asks "Do you know...?" questions similar to those in the dialogue.

Communication Activities

A. Do you remember?

Do you remember what you did on your first date?

EASY RIDER
NOW SHOWING

We went to a movie.

B. Occupations

A pilot.

Michelle's Team 6

Emel's Team 3

A pilot has to know how to

A pilot has to know how to speak English.

C. Hidden treasure

Photocopiable

20 Consolidation Exercises

1. Know

a. He knows *where his teeth are.*

b. She knows

c. He knows

d. He doesn't know

e. He knows

f. They don't know

2. Wonder

I wonder why *countries fight each other.*

I wonder when

I wonder who

I wonder where

Questionnaire

At work/school

I have to know what

I have to know when

I have to know how

I have to know where

Do you remember who your first English teacher was?

Do you remember who your best friend was when you were six?

Do you remember where you use to play with your friends when you were a child?

Do you remember what you dreamed about last night?

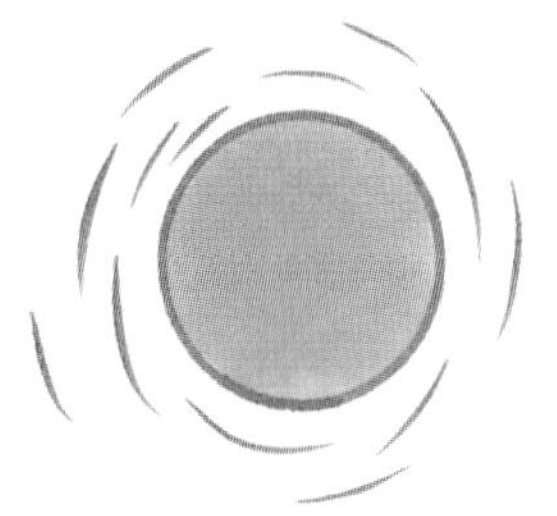

Conditionals • 1 •

Lead-in If you play, a lot of people will come

Michelle: Marc, I need your help.

Marc: What's the matter?

Michelle: I'm organizing a charity concert, and I'd like you to play.

Marc: I'm too busy.

Michelle: If you play, a lot of people will come, and we'll raise a lot of money.

Marc: I never play in charity concerts.

Michelle: Please, help us, Marc! If we raise $5,000, we'll be able to buy food for hundreds of people.

Marc: Who else is going to play?

Michelle: I'm not sure yet. But I think Paula's going to play the piano, Kim will probably play bass, and I hope Sachiko will play drums. So, if you sing and play lead guitar, it'll be a great concert.

Marc: If I play with Paula, Kim, and Sachiko, it'll be bad for my image. My manager will never agree.

Language Builder

If Michelle studies hard, she'll pass her exams.

If Manuel works overtime, he'll be able to save a lot of money.

Controlled practice If she studies hard ...

If she studies hard, ______________________

____

____

Follow-up practice If you marry me, I'll work very hard

Romeo: If you marry me, I'll buy you beautiful clothes and expensive jewelry.

Juliet: Where will you get the money?

Romeo: If you marry me, I'll work very hard and I'll earn a lot of money.

Juliet: So, I'll have to stay home and do all the housework!

Romeo: No! If you marry me, I'll do the housework, too. I'll cook and wash your clothes.

Juliet: You don't have to cook them! Just washing them is enough.

Pair practice

If the students are of the opposite sex, Student A should try to persuade Student B to marry him/her, using the pattern "If ...". If the students are of the same sex, they can play the roles of famous people of different sexes.

A. Vacations

B. Prompts

C. Complete the sentence

Photocopiable

21 Consolidation Exercises

1. Chains

a. If I stay up late tonight, I'll be tired tomorrow.
If I'm tired tomorrow, ________________.
If ________________.
________________.
____

b. If I speak English fluently, ________________.
If ________________.
________________.
________________.

2. If she works hard ...

a. If she works hard, she'll get a lot of money.
____

b. ________________

c. ________________

d. ________________

Questionnaire

What will you do tomorrow ...

if it rains?
____

if the weather's nice?
____

if it's extremely hot?
____

What will you do on your next vacation ...

if it rains?
____

if the weather's nice?
____

if it's extremely hot?
____

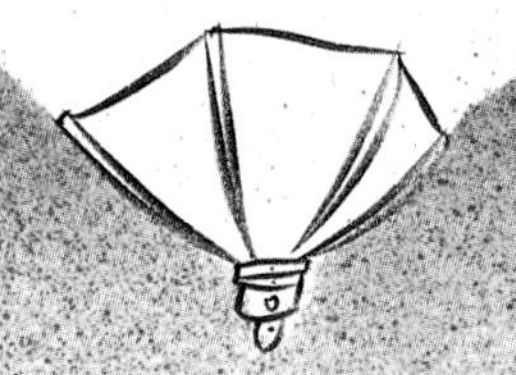

Conditionals 2

Lead-in

If it isn't raining, I ride my bike

Marc: Where are you staying?

Emel: On Seventh Street.

Marc: That's quite far away. How do you get to school?

Emel: If it isn't raining, I ride my bike.

Marc: How long does it take?

Emel: If I leave home early, it takes about forty minutes. But if I'm late, there's too much traffic and it takes longer.

Marc: Um ... Would you like to dance?

Emel: Only if you play in Michelle's charity concert.

Marc: Michelle sent you, didn't she?

Emel: ... Well, thank you for the drink. I have to be going now.

Marc: Wait! ... OK. I'll play!

Emel: And if you give all the money from your next album to charity, I'll go dancing with you every night next week.

Language Builder

If/When David gets up early, he goes jogging before breakfast.

If/When Sachiko isn't busy, she likes to practice the drums.

Controlled practice What do they do on Sundays?

1

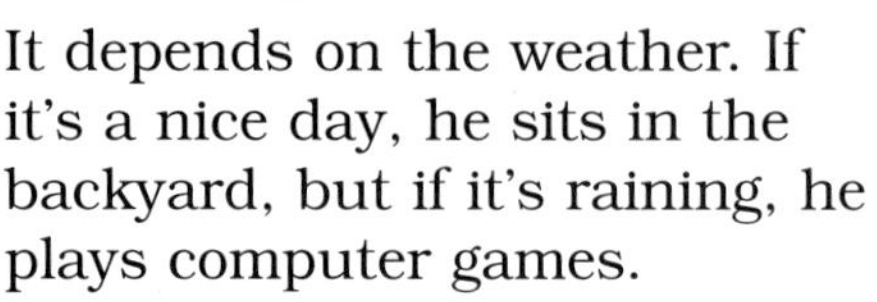

It depends on the weather. If it's a nice day, he sits in the backyard, but if it's raining, he plays computer games.

2

It depends on what ____________

3

It depends on how ____________

Follow-up practice It depends on how tired I am

Bruce: What do you usually do on Sundays?

Boris: It depends on how tired I am. When I'm very tired, I stay home and watch TV. But when I'm feeling energetic, I usually go hunting.

Bruce: What do you usually hunt?

Boris: It depends on what I want to eat. If I feel like fresh food, I hunt for something in the supermarket. But if I feel like frozen food, I look for a mammoth.

Pair practice

Student A asks Student B a question which is likely to have more than one answer (e.g. "What kind of food do you like?", or "What do you do in the evenings?"). Student B answers using the pattern "It depends on ... . If/When ..., but if/when ..." The teacher may have to write the framework and some starting questions on the board.

A. Tennis
If I feel bored, I telephone my friends.
If I telephone my friends, I talk for a long time.
If I talk for a long time, I lose my voice.
B. Answering *If* ...
What's your favorite sport?
If the weather's nice, I like playing golf. But if it's raining, I like playing tennis.
Manuel 3 Sunee 4
Kim 5 Sachiko 6
C. It depends on ...
Photocopiable
Where would you like to take a vacation?
It depends on how busy I am. If I'm very busy, I'd like to go to Hawaii for a few days. But if I have more time, I'd like to go hiking in the Andes.
Where would you like to take a vacation?
It depends on how busy I am.

22 Consolidation Exercises

1. Answering *If* ...

What do you do on Tuesday evenings?
If ______

What time do you get up?
If ______

What do you have for breakfast?
If ______

What TV shows do you like?
If ______

2. What does she do in the evenings?

a. If she's feeling ______ tired,
she watches TV.

b. ______ sociable,
______

c. ______ energetic,
______

3. It depends on the/how/what ...

What do you do on Sundays?
It depends on the ______
It depends on how ______
It depends on what ______

Do you work/study hard?
It depends on the ______
It depends on how ______
It depends on what ______

Questionnaire

What kind of movies do you like?
It depends on ______.
If ______,
but if ______
______.

What time do you go to bed?
It depends on ______.
If ______,
but if ______
______.

Do you do much exercise?
It depends on ______.
If ______,
but if ______
______.

Do you enjoy your English lessons?
It depends on ______.
If ______,
but if ______
______.

Giving reasons 23

Lead-in Because, if I can speak English ...

Sachiko: Why are you learning English?

Sunee: Because, if I can speak English well, I may be able to work for a multi-national company.

Sachiko: Why do you want to do that?

Sunee: Because, if I work for a multi-national company, I'll probably get a lot more chances to travel.

Sachiko: I travel all the time. It's very tiring!

Sunee: So, why do you do it?

Sachiko: That's a good question.

Emel: Why do you smoke so much?

Marc: It helps me think.

Emel: And why do you drink so much?

Marc: It helps me relax.

Emel: But smoking and drinking are bad for your health.

Marc: Why are you so worried about me?

Emel: I'm not worried. I just think you're stupid.

Language Builder

Kim plays a lot of golf because it helps him relax.

Paula doesn't like using a computer because it gives her a headache.

David drinks a lot of coffee because it stops him falling asleep in class.

Marc doesn't like studying hard because it makes him very tired.

Controlled practice Why?

1

Why does he watch vampire movies?
It helps him relax.

2

Why does he go jogging?
________________ stops
____

3

Why doesn't he sit under apple trees?
________________ gives
________________ a ________________

Follow-up practice Why do you train so hard?

Juliet: Why are you so strong?
Bruce: Because I train hard every day.
Juliet: Why do you train so hard?
Bruce: Because I want to win an Olympic medal.
Juliet: Why do you want to win an Olympic medal?
Bruce: Because, if I win an Olympic medal, I'll be rich and famous.
Juliet: You are so strong! And you are so ambitious! You look like my fourth husband!
Bruce: How many husbands have you had?
Juliet: Only three.

Pair practice

Student A asks Student B a "Why?" question (e.g. "Why are you learning English?"), and follows up by asking a succession of further "Why?" questions in response to each of Student B's answers.

A. Why?

B. Why don't you?

C. City planning

Photocopiable

23 Consolidation Exercises

1. Why do we study?

a. 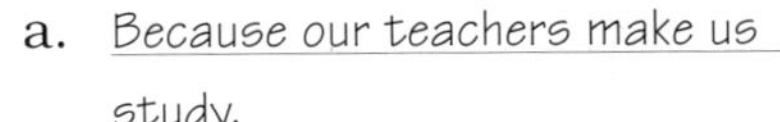
Because our teachers make us study.

b.

c.

d.

e.

f.

2. Three reasons

Why do people have cars?

1.
2.
3.

Why do people get up in the morning?

1.
2.
3.

Questionnaire

Do you smoke? Why?

Do you stay up late? Why?

Do you listen to music a lot? Why?

Do you eat out a lot? Why?

Do you often go abroad? Why?

Do you walk to work/school? Why?

Reported speech •2• 24

Lead-in Ask them if they are tired

... Next we have some sensational news! Last week, we reported that Carmen and Emel, two unknown tennis players, had beaten last year's champions in the Palm Sands Ladies Doubles Tournament. When we interviewed them, Carmen told us that they would win the tournament, but we didn't believe her. Today we have a live interview with Carmen and Emel, the new ladies doubles champions ...

Presenter: Ask them if they are tired.

Reporter: Are you tired?

Emel: Yes, very tired.

Presenter: Ask them if they are pleased.

Reporter: Are you pleased?

Carmen: No, we aren't.

Presenter: Ask Carmen why she isn't pleased.

Reporter: Why aren't you pleased?

Carmen: Because I'm tired, and you're asking too many questions.

Language Builder

A: Ask ____________ if ____________.
B: ____________________________?
C: Yes/No ____________________________.

A: Ask ____________ what/where ... ____________.
B: What/Where ... ____________________________?
C: ____________________________.

Controlled practice What did they say?

1a 

He told her that she had won.
He said that she had won.

1b 

1c 

2a 

He told them to sit down.

2b 

He asked ______________________

2c 

She invited ______________________

Follow-up practice Tell them to park in the parking lot

Mrs. Shakespeare:	How did that thing get into my kitchen?
Shakespeare:	They said they turned left in the living room.
Mrs. Shakespeare:	Well, tell them to park in the parking lot down the street. Anyway, who are they?
Shakespeare:	They said they come from another planet.
Mrs Shakespeare:	Oh, they're foreigners.
Zork:	Do you think they're intelligent?
Glug:	I don't think so.
Zork:	Ask them a difficult question.
Glug:	What's 11 x 7 ÷ 2.5?
Mrs. Shakespeare:	Are you crazy? William, tell them to stay here. I'm going to get the police.

Groups of three practice

Student A: a scientist. Student B: a robot. Student C: an operator.
Student A gives instructions to Student B through Student C, using the pattern "Tell him/her to ..."(e.g. "Tell her to open the window."). Student A should remain in one place and give instructions quietly to Student C.

A. Interviewing a superstar
Where do you live?
HOLLYWOOD
In Hollywood.
Ask her where she lives.
She said she lives in Hollywood.
B. Drawing by remote control
Tell him to draw a cow at the bottom right.
Draw a cow at the bottom on the right.
C. Commands
Photocopiable
Tell the player on your left to count backwards from twenty to one.

24 Consolidation Exercises

1. What did they say?

a. She asked him if he was

busy.

b. He told ______________________

c. She invited ______________________

d. He told ______________________

e. She told ______________________

f. He asked ______________________

2. I'd like ...

I'd like to ask my boss/teacher to

____

I'd like to ask the president of my country to

____

I'd like to ask my favorite movie star to

____

I'd like to ask people all over the world to

____

Questionnaire

What have people told you to do?

My mother used to tell me to get up early.

a. ______________________

b. ______________________

c. ______________________

d. ______________________

Conditionals •3• 25

Lead-in If I were the President ...

Kim: Taxes are much too high! If I were the President, I'd cut taxes by at least 50 percent.

Michelle: You're worrying too much. If I were your boss, I'd tell you to take a vacation.

Kim: I guess you're right.

Michelle: What would you do if you had a long vacation?

Kim: I'd go back to Cheju Island, relax on the beach ... and forget about taxes.

Sachiko: What would you do if you had a lot of money?

David: I'd start a professional soccer team.

Sachiko: Soccer! You only think about soccer!

David: Well, what would you do?

Sachiko: I'd buy two tickets for a round-the-world cruise.

David: Why two tickets?

Sachiko: For you and me, of course.

David: Oh.

Language Builder

If David was/were a woman, he'd/he would understand Sachiko better.

If Paula had more money, she'd/she would build an art studio.

If Manuel worked harder, he'd/he would earn more money.

Controlled practice — If they were ...

1

If she were a flower,
she'd like to be a rose.

2

3

4

5

Follow-up practice — If you were on a desert island ...

Reporter: If you were on a desert island, what would you like to have with you?

Shakespeare: I'd like a word processor so I could write a play and a helicopter so I could go home.

Romeo: I'd like a guitar so I could compose some love songs and a yacht so I could sail home.

Boris: I'd like a spear so I could go hunting, and a TV because I'd be bored after the others went home.

Pair practice

The students take turns to say something they would like to have on a desert island and give a reason.

A. Sentence building
If I had a million dollars, I'd buy a big house.
If I had a million dollars, I'd buy a big house and travel around the world.
B. Elimination
I'd take a radio.
I'd take a radio, too.
C. Guess the situation
Photocopiable
I'd be lonely.
If you lived alone?
No! ... I'd wear a spacesuit.
If you were an astronaut?
If you lived on the moon

25 Consolidation Exercises

1. Chains

a. If I were a dog, I'd eat dog food.

If I ate dog food, I'd be sick.

If I were sick, I'd go to hospital.

b. If I were Australian,

c. If I were a man/woman,

d. If I were a banana,

2. What would he take to a desert island and why?

He'd take a radio.

Questionnaire

What would you do if ...

you were president of your country?

you had no money or home?

another country attacked your country?

you saw a ghost?

Passives 26

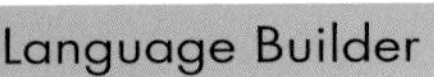

He was murdered in this room

Lead-in

Paula: This book was written by a local historian and there's a chapter on our house.

Lee: What does it say?

Paula: It says the house was built in 1845.

Lee: 1845! We were told it was sixty years old!

Paula: It was designed by a famous architect.

Lee: So, why is the kitchen on the third floor?

Paula: The third floor was added by a crazy owner in 1876. But in 1877, he was murdered in this room by his wife.

Lee: Maybe because he put the kitchen on the third floor.

Paula: It isn't funny! Listen! Since then, three husbands have been killed by their wives in this room.

Lee: Let's go and sleep downstairs.

Language Builder

The electric light was invented by Thomas Edison.

Gravity was discovered by Isaac Newton.

Romeo and Juliet was written by William Shakespeare.

The Moonlight Sonata was composed by Beethoven.

Controlled practice Inventions and discoveries ...

1 The Mona Lisa was painted by Leonardo da Vinci.

2 Tess ______________ ______________ Thomas Hardy.

3 The telephone ______________ ______________ Bell.

4 Star Wars ______________ ______________ George Lucas.

5 Swan Lake ______________ ______________ Tchaikovsky.

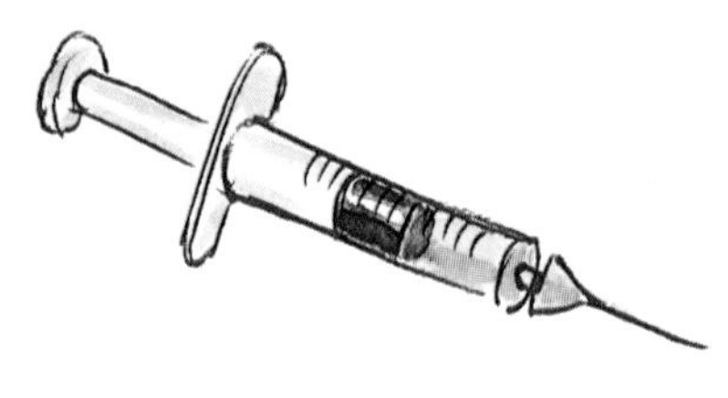

6 Penicillin ______________ ______________ Fleming.

Follow-up practice My egg should be fried

Princess: My egg should be fried not boiled!

Frog: And my soup should have more flies in it!

Waiter: I'm very sorry, sir. We're short of flies at the moment.

Princess: And my hamburger should be cooked more! It's almost raw!

Waiter: I'll bring you another one ma'am.

Princess: Will it be very long?

Waiter: No ma'am. I think it'll be round.

Pair practice

Student A: a waiter. Student B: a customer ordering a meal.
Student B orders a meal, and then complains about it.

A. Leaving the room
I think this bag has been moved from over there.
B. What's going to happen?
I think a time machine will be invented.
Science
Manuel's Team 6
Sachiko's Team 9
C. Quiz
Photocopiable
When was the jet engine invented?
QUIZ
QUIZ
QUIZ

26 Consolidation Exercises

1. General knowledge

a. *JAWS*

was directed by Spielberg.

b. *Hamlet*

c. The electric light

d. *The Moonlight Sonata*

e. *Yesterday*

f. North America

g. Gravity

h. Halley's Comet

2. How many times ...

have you been invited to parties?

About thirty times.

have you been robbed?

have you been sent love letters?

have you been given presents?

have you been kissed?

have you been arrested?

Questionnaire

How should your town/city be improved?

a.

b.

How should your school/office be improved?

a.

b.

How should your English lessons be improved?

a.

b.

How should the world be improved?

a.

b.

Relative clauses

Lead-in I don't like people who ...

Manuel: Have you heard of Sam Stapleton?

Carmen: You mean the tennis coach who's trained three Wimbledon champions?

Manuel: Yes, that's right. Pete Pampas said he's interested in coaching you.

Carmen: I heard that he's very strict. I don't like people who are too strict.

Manuel: He's very successful.

Carmen: I want to be coached by somebody who's kind and patient. Anyway, I'm too busy, and I'm sure we can't afford to pay for his lessons.

Manuel: Don't worry about anything. I've found somebody who can help with the housework and I'm going to work overtime to pay for everything. And if the coach is too strict, we'll find somebody else.

Carmen: Thank you, Manuel.

Language Builder

Kim doesn't like people who/that drive too fast.

Manuel doesn't like animals which/that make a lot of noise.

Sunee doesn't like movies which/that are violent.

Controlled practice Dislikes

1

Carmen's dog doesn't like dogs which/that are bigger than him.

2

3

4

Follow-up practice What's a getaway car?

Glug: What's this?
Policeman: It's a getaway car.
Glug: What's a getaway car?
Policeman: It's a car which a bank robber escapes in.
Glug: What's a bank robber?
Policeman: It's a person who steals money from a bank.
Glug: What's a bank?
Policeman: It's a place where we keep money.

Ouch!

Glug: What's that?
Robber: It's a thing which I hit policemen with when they stop me getting into my getaway car.

Pair practice

Student A: an alien. Student B: him/herself.
Student A asks what things, places, types of people are. Student B explains using the patterns "It's a thing/something which/that ...", "It's a person/somebody who/that ...", "It's a place/somewhere where/which/that ...".

Communication Activities 27

A. Switch chairs

B. Making crosswords

What's a good clue for "table"?

How about – "a thing which we put things on"?

C. Find somebody who

photocopiable

Have you been to Singapore?

No, I haven't.

27 Consolidation Exercises

1. What's a ...

What's a chair?

It's a thing which we sit on.

What's a teacher?

What's a park?

What's a pen?

What's a pilot?

What's a station?

2. Crossword

Across

2. A thing which we wash our bodies in.
4.
5.
7.
10.
11.

Down

1.
3.
4.
6.
8.
9.

Questionnaire

I like people who

I don't like people

I like animals

I don't like animals

I like cities

I don't like cities

I like teachers

I don't like teachers

Should have • Would have 28

Lead-in You should have telephoned us!

Marc: I'm sorry I'm late. I overslept.

Sachiko: You shouldn't have stayed up so late last night!

Paula: And you should have telephoned us! We've been waiting for nearly two hours!

Marc: If my alarm had gone off, I would have been here on time.

Sachiko: If you hadn't drunk so much last night, you would have remembered to set your alarm!

Kim: Let's stop fighting! The concert's tomorrow, and we have to do a lot of practicing. Michelle told me that she's sold a thousand tickets, so we'd better play well.

Marc: A thousand tickets! We should have started practicing hours ago!

Language Builder

If Lee had stayed in Shanghai, he wouldn't have met Paula.

If Marc had studied harder, he would have gone to college.

If Carmen hadn't got married, she might have become a famous lawyer.

If Sachiko hadn't become a stewardess, she might have played in a rock band.

Controlled practice

They should have ...

1 

2 

3 

He should have trained more.

4 

5 

6 

Follow-up practice

It could be a spaceship

Zork: What do you think it is?

Glug: It could be a spaceship.

Zork: Yes, it doesn't have round wheels, so it can't be a car.

Glug: We'd better examine it. Humans might have discovered how to break the light barrier.

Zork: No, they can't have done that yet!

Glug: It's possible. Simple designs are usually the most sophisticated. ... Um ... Excuse me. How about exchanging your machine for ours?

Boris: Sure, if you like.

Zork: But, Glug, how will we get home?

Glug: In his machine, of course.

Pair practice

Both students are aliens. They examine things around them and suggest what they might or can't be. The teacher or other students could also supply some unusual objects for the students to speculate about.

A. Pirates

B. If I'd been born ...

C. Unusual views

Photocopiable

28 Consolidation Exercises

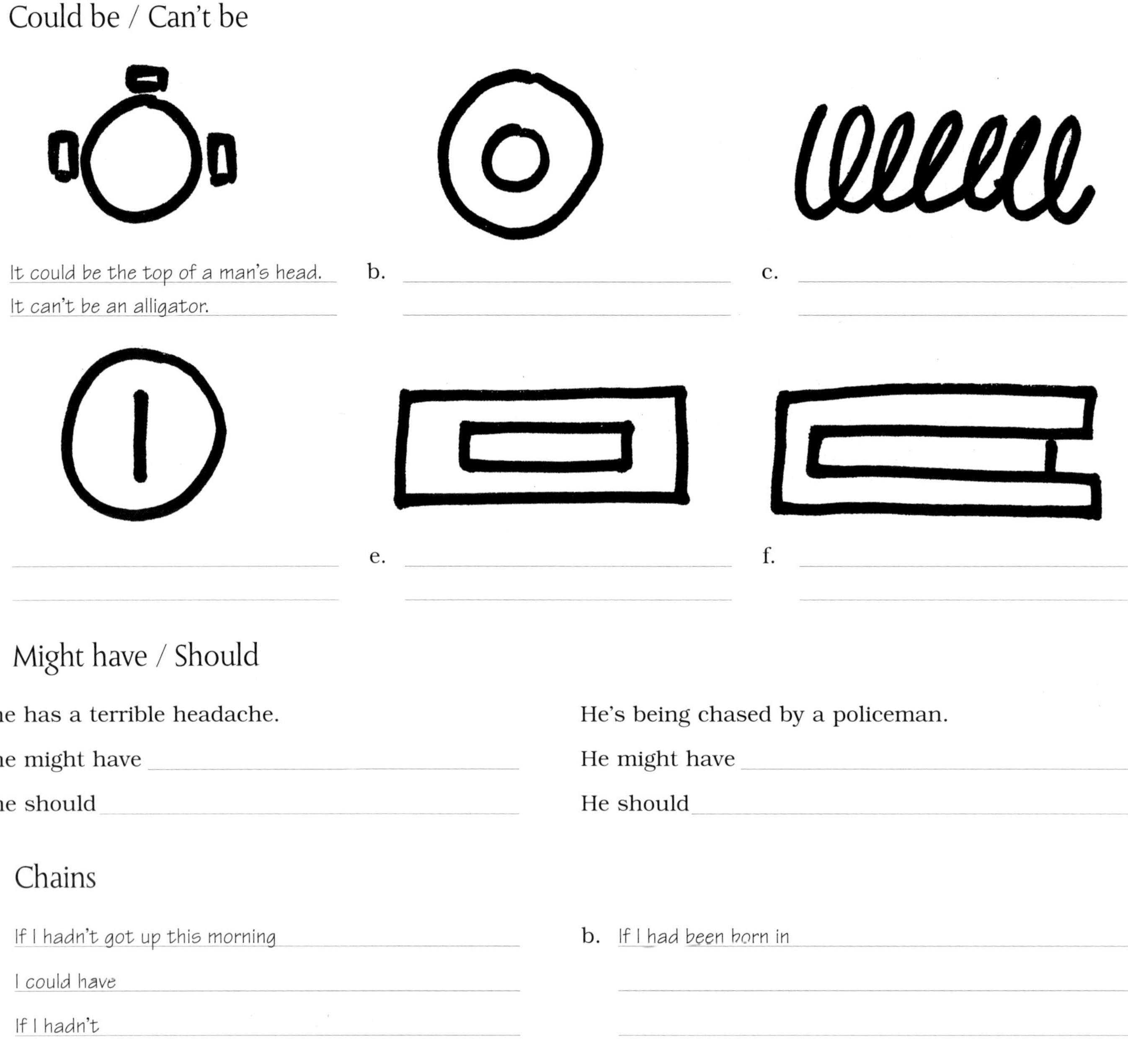

1. Could be / Can't be

a. It could be the top of a man's head.
It can't be an alligator.

b.

c.

d.

e.

f.

2. Might have / Should

She has a terrible headache.

She might have

She should

He's being chased by a policeman.

He might have

He should

3. Chains

a. If I hadn't got up this morning
I could have
If I hadn't

b. If I had been born in

Questionnaire

When I was younger ...

I could

I couldn't

I should have

I shouldn't have

If I had

If I had

Impressions 29

Lead-in You must have worked very hard!

Reporter: The concert seems to be going very well.

Michelle: Yes, everybody seems to be enjoying it.

Reporter: How much money have you raised?

Michelle: $30,000.

Reporter: $30,000! You must be very pleased. You must have worked very hard!

Michelle: A lot of people have worked hard.

Reporter: Yes, but it must have been very difficult to persuade Marc Delon to play. He never does anything for charity.

Michelle: He seems to have changed a bit recently. It looks like he's going to give all the money from his next album to charity.

Reporter: Can I report that?

Michelle: Sure. Then he'll have to do it.

Language Builder

Carmen and Emel must be very excited.

Sachiko, Kim, Marc, and Paula must have practiced very hard.

David always seems (to be) very serious.

Manuel seems to have become less selfish.

Controlled practice It looks like ...

1 

It looks like it's going to rain.

2 

3 

4 

5 

6 

Follow-up practice Your hair is like silk

Shakespeare:	You dance like a butterfly on a summer's day.
Mrs. Shakespeare:	You're very romantic tonight. Have you been drinking?
Shakespeare:	Your hair is like silk.
Mrs. Shakespeare:	It feels like spaghetti.
Shakespeare:	It blows in the wind like daffodils in spring.
Mrs. Shakespeare:	Maybe the window's open.
Shakespeare:	Your eyes are like the deep blue ocean.
Mrs. Shakespeare:	That's my tinted contact lenses.
Shakespeare:	Your teeth are like stars.
Mrs. Shakespeare:	Like stars?
Shakespeare:	Yes. They come out at night.

Pair practice

Student A says the name of a famous person and challenges Student B to make five sentences about him/her. Each of Student B's answers must include a simile.

A. Pictures of people

B. Like/Look like

C. Must/Must have

Photocopiable

29 Consolidation Exercises

1. Seems

a. He seems (to be) very happy.

b.

c.

2. There seem(s) to be

a. There seems to be more crime than before.

b.

c.

d.

3. Must / Must have

He's running to catch a train.

He must

He must have

She's sleeping in her office.

She must

She must have

4. Like

He works very hard.

He works like an ant.

She sings beautifully.

She sleeps too much.

He eats too much.

Questionnaire

What do you think is going to happen to you?

It looks like

It looks like

It looks like

What do you think is going to happen in your country?

It looks like

It looks like

It looks like

Discussions 30

Lead-in In Brazil we think ...

Marc: You played very well.

Paula: Thank you.

Marc: You don't play as well as French musicians, of course. French pianists play with more soul. And bass players in France don't play so many notes.

Paula: I don't care how French musicians play! In Brazil, we think rhythm is important. And I'm sure Kim knows more about playing bass than you do. He's a very famous musician in Korea.

Marc: You never said you were famous, Kim.

Paula: Maybe Korean people are more modest than French people!

Kim: It depends on the person. Anyway, I usually play classical music, so Marc is probably right.

Sachiko: Why don't you come and teach in Japan?

David: I don't speak any Japanese, and I don't understand Japanese customs.

Sachiko: Don't worry! I'll help you. ... First, let me show you how to use chopsticks. You put both of them in the same hand like this. Then you pick up the raw octopus like this.

David: Raw octopus! Are you sure I'll be all right in Japan?

Language Builder

In Brazil, people love watching and playing soccer.

In Italy, people eat a lot of pasta.

In Japan, people take off their shoes before entering a house.

Controlled practice World problems

1

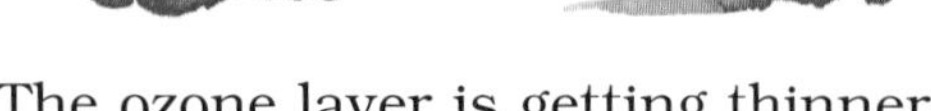

The ozone layer is getting thinner.

2

3

4

Follow-up practice You aren't very intelligent

Bruce: What's your impression of the Earth?

Zork: It's a very beautiful planet. But it's in great danger! The ozone layer is getting thinner, and the balance of nature has been lost.

Princess: What's your impression of humans?

Zork: You aren't very intelligent. You're always fighting each other! You should learn to live together in peace. Then you can solve the ozone layer problem, and restore the balance of nature.

Romeo: Do you think we can succeed?

Zork: I'm not sure, but I hope so. Then you can help us destroy our enemies, the three-legged aliens from the Milky Way.

Pair practice

The students take turns to ask each other's impressions of various countries around the world, using the pattern "What's your impression of ...?"

A. Local customs

B. Similarities and differences

C. Questionnaire (Units 16–30)

Photocopiable

30 Consolidation Exercises

1. What's your impression of ...

Canada

Brazil

Egypt

China

Germany

India

2. Special customs in your country

a.

b.

c.

d.

Questionnaire

What's your impression of humans?

How can we all live together in peace?

How can we restore the balance of nature?

Do you think we can succeed?

Verb Chart

	Past tense	Past participle		Past tense	Past participle
ask	asked	asked	lose		
be	was/were	been	love		
become	became	become	make		
break	broke	broken	meet		
bring	brought	brought	play		
buy	bought	bought	put		
call			read		
catch			ride		
climb			run		
come			say		
cut			see		
do			sell		
drink			send		
drive			shut		
eat			sing		
enjoy			sit		
fight			sleep		
find			speak		
fly			stand		
forget			stay		
get			study		
give			swim		
go			take		
hate			teach		
have			tell		
hear			think		
hit			try		
hurt			walk		
jump			want		
know			watch		
leave			wear		
like			win		
live			work		
look			write		

Answers:
call-called-called, catch-caught-caught, climb-climbed-climbed, come-came-come, cut-cut-cut, do-did-done, drink-drank-drunk, drive-drove-driven, eat-ate-eaten, enjoy-enjoyed-enjoyed, fight-fought-fought, find-found-found, fly-flew-flown, forget-forgot-forgotten, get-got-got/gotten, give-gave-given, go-went-gone, hate-hated-hated, have-had-had, hear-heard-heard, hit-hit-hit, hurt-hurt-hurt, jump-jumped-jumped, know-knew-known, leave-left-left, like-liked-liked, live-lived-lived, look-looked-looked, lose-lost-lost, love-loved-loved, make-made-made, meet-met-met, play-played-played, put-put-put, read-read-read, ride-rode-ridden, run-ran-run, say-said-said, see-saw-seen, sell-sold-sold, send-sent-sent, shut-shut-shut, sing-sang-sung, sit-sat-sat, sleep-slept-slept, speak-spoke-spoken, stand-stood-stood, stay-stayed-stayed, study-studied-studied, swim-swam-swum, take-took-taken, teach-taught-taught, tell-told-told, think-thought-thought, try-tried-tried, walk-walked-walked, want-wanted-wanted, watch-watched-watched, wear-wore-worn, win-won-won, work-worked-worked, write-wrote-written.

Heinemann English Language Teaching
A division of Heinemann Publishers (Oxford) Ltd.
Halley Court, Jordan Hill, Oxford OX2 8EJ

OXFORD MADRID ATHENS PARIS FLORENCE
PRAGUE SÃO PAULO CHICAGO MELBOURNE
AUCKLAND SINGAPORE TOKYO IBADAN
GABORONE JOHANNESBURG
PORTSMOUTH (NH)

First published 1995

Illustrated by: Gary Andrews, Leendert Jan Vis, Peter Richardson, Celia Witchard, Richard Draper

The publishers would like to thank Billy Woolfolk, Hironaka Educational Language Institute, Japan; Carl Bender, GEM International Academy, Japan; Peter Collier, ELSI, Taiwan; Tely Kalambaheti, ECC, Thailand; Ginger Ropp, Tokyo Language Institute, Japan; Wendy Shyu, GRAM English Center, Taiwan; Piroska Szabó, CEL-LEP, Brazil.

The author would like to thank everyone at Heinemann for their hard work and support, especially Valerie Gossage, Alix Harrower, Denise Cripps, Vaughan Jones, Barton Armstrong, Hajime Shishido, Richard Kemp, and Mike Esplen.

All the teachers and staff at David English House who have contributed so many useful suggestions, especially David Evans and Richard Walker.

Communicate Level 1 consists of:

Student's Book	435 26108 8	(Japanese edition)
Student's Book	435 26116 9	(International edition)
Workbook	435 26109 6	
Teacher's Book	435 26110 X	
Cassette	435 26111 8	
CD	435 26117 7	

Communicate Level 2 consists of:

Student's Book	435 26112 6
Workbook	435 26113 4
Teacher's Book	435 26114 2
Cassette	435 26115 0
CD	435 26118 5

Split editions:

Student's Book 1A	435 26119 3
Student's Book 1B	435 26120 7
Workbook 1A	435 26121 5
Workbook 1B	435 26122 3
Cassette 1A	435 26123 1
Cassette 1B	435 26124 X

Student's Book 2A	435 26134 7
Student's Book 2B	435 26135 5
Workbook 2A	435 26136 3
Workbook 2B	435 26137 1
Cassette 2A	435 26138 X
Cassette 2B	435 26139 8

Printed and bound in Spain by Cayfosa

95 96 97 98 99 10 9 8 7 6 5 4 3 2 1